Kiss Goodbye

The Story of God's Presence in the Dark Night

Deb Watson

Acknowledgments

Jesus, You are the Alpha and Omega, Who is, and Who was, and Who is to come, the Beginning and the End, the First and the Last, and it is my privilege to give You all the honor and glory. In You, all things are possible. Thank you for making this book possible.

I personally invite you, the reader, into the intimate recesses of our family, as we have grappled with an unthinkable loss. My hope is that by peeling back the veil of grief others facing similar trials, might be encouraged to seek first and foremost, God Himself, as the answer to their needs. The primary purpose of this book is not to expound on the pain of loss, although very real, but rather to share the story of God's presence and faithfulness in the midst of such pain. Without God, there would be no story to tell.

I am especially grateful to my husband and daughters for the freedom they have granted me in exposing, not only my deep anguish, but theirs, as well.

My husband, Mark—my best friend, my soul mate—how can I adequately thank you for your support and encouragement in making this book a reality? The finished manuscript is truly the product of the endless hours of mutual conversation. I simply say thank you—I love you so much!

My precious daughters, Jennifer, Laurie, Christy, Keri and Sarah—you gave me so many reasons to keep on living, even when everything within me wanted to die. My anchor in Cathy's death was her faith in Christ and it is a great blessing to see that same faith in Christ mature in each of you. Thank you for the joy you continue to bring to my life.

My son-in-laws, Joe, Rhody, Jared, Travis and Justin—each of you is like a son to me. You are indeed a blessing, and I am deeply indebted to each of you for the loving way you care for my daughters and grandchildren. Thank you.

My grandchildren, Kaitlyn, Savannah, Ryan, Reese, Tyler, Max, Cameron, Lauren, Leif and Liza—what a great joy you bring to my life, thank you! *...And the babies we await with such expectancy*—you are God's proof that life goes on.

My parents, who modeled unconditional love and raised me in a home that honored the name of Jesus—how do I begin to thank you for the impact you have had on my life? Your encouragement has helped me stay focused and I so appreciate your support in getting this book into print.

Dwight Edwards, who I knew first as an author, but now have the joy of calling friend—I thank you for your encouragement and insight. It is such an honor to have you write the foreword to this book. God has uniquely gifted you, enabling you to write with such a provocative style. Your words come off the page and into the human heart. You inspire me! Thank you for your kind words.

Pastor Scott—thank you for the many hours you provided a safe place and listening ear. You will never know how richly God has used you in my life.

To my dear friends, Mary and Brenda, who walked closely beside me through this deep valley—thank you from the bottom of my heart. Your friendship has deeply blessed me.

To those of you in our small group, Larry, Carol, Jared, Christy, Phil, Michelle, Julio, Heather, Greg and

Kristina—your encouragement and prayers were vital to this undertaking. Thank you.

To my church family at Warroad Baptist Church—your prayers and acts of kindness carried us through some very deep waters. Thank you.

To those special friends of whom there are too many to list—thank you for taking the time to read the draft of this book and encouraging me to press on.

To the staff of BookSurge.com—thank you for the direction and encouragement you provided. A special thank you to my first editor, Laura Matthews—your kind words and personal identification gave me the courage to tell our story.

To Carol Hallan—who graciously proofread this text and offered her valued opinion on grammar and punctuation. Thank you so very much.

To Ilene Olson, Nature's Photography, Inc. who was the photographer responsible for the picture that inspired *Kiss Goodbye* and who graciously granted me full copyright use of all the photographs she had taken of Cathy. Thank you.

To my daughter, Cathy, who was the first in our immediate family to enter the gates of heaven, how do I begin to thank you? What can I say? Words all fall short. You inspire me daily by the testimony of your life. I love you and miss you!

Lastly, Jesus, because You are the Alpha and Omega, Who is, and Who was, and Who is to come, the Beginning and the End, the First and the Last. I fall on my knees in praise and adoration. You are my Stronghold, my Redeemer, my Deliverer, my Salvation; without You, I would have no story to tell and no hope to sustain me.

Table of Contents

Foreword

I am a huge fan of short forewords. Not because I think they are unimportant, but primarily because I don't think there is a need for an extended description of how good the entrée is…the first bite will take care of that. And so I want to introduce you to one of the best books I have read in several years, and then quickly get out of the way, so you can begin enjoying the fabulous meal awaiting you in these chapters.

Let me begin by introducing you to an amazing couple – Mark and Deb Watson and their six daughters: Jennifer, Laurie, Catherine, Christy, Keri, and Sarah. Catherine, or as she was best known – Cathy, is the central figure of this book. But she isn't the central message. The central message is that there is a God Who can take His people through the most piercingly difficult, excruciatingly painful, utterly confusing, seemingly hopeless times in their lives and bring them out to a wealthier place. Not overnight. Not easily. Never pain-free. But genuinely. Deeply. And most of all, supernaturally.

Mark and Deb are a wonderful couple I met a few years ago when they graciously invited me to come speak at their church retreat. This came at a time in my life when I had just come out of a very dark night of the soul and was reeling from some huge failures on my part. Wondering if God would ever use me again, their invitation was one of His first whispers that He was not through with me. You never forget the first people willing to take a chance on you after you have failed. Mark and Deb will always have a special place in my heart for being among those people.

They are a fun couple, a little crazy at times, and above all else – astonishingly authentic. They are the real deal in spades. You will see this throughout the book. Deb does an amazing job of sharing what must be one of the most (if not the most) difficult traumas in life – the death of a child. I so appreciate her candor, raw honesty, and courage in describing the entire ordeal. I shake my head in awe of their responses and dependence upon our Savior.

But above all, I am most tempted to fall to my knees and worship my God in new ways. Their responses to Cathy's death can only be explained by resurrection power. Their outlook can only be understood by the eternal perspective Christ alone provides. Their God-empowered perseverance encourages me to take the next faltering step God has placed before me.

I read the book in one sitting. I couldn't put it down. I don't think you will be able to either. So I invite you to take up and read. And enjoy. And, most of all, worship.

By Dwight Edwards
Pastor, Author, Speaker

Dedication

IN MEMORY OF

JOHNNY ALEXANDER STOLL

SEPTEMBER 28, 2004

*Johnny Alexander
You took your first breath in heaven
and I believe you are enjoying fullness
at the feet of Jesus.*

*Johnny, I love you.
Cathy, please rock my little friend in heaven!*

*On this side of heaven
God grants us unique opportunities
to bless and be blessed.*

*Pastor Scott and Linda
God placed you in our lives
for such a time as this.
What a blessed gift!*

*And what an honor
He bestowed upon us
to in turn walk alongside you
through your dark night.*

*Our children Cathy and Johnny
have become our greatest teachers
of what truly matters.*

*Praise God for His Indescribable Gift.
We have this hope
as an anchor for the soul,
firm and secure.
The hope of eternal life.*

In the early hours of September 28, 2004, we received the heartbreaking news that our Pastor and his wife had given birth to a stillborn son. Only four years earlier, Pastor Scott had conducted Cathy's funeral, now Mark would conduct the funeral for Johnny Alexander. The intertwining of our paths gave us the opportunity to share the comfort we had received from God during our own dark night.

A Little About Me

Not that we are adequate in ourselves to consider anything as coming from ourselves, but our adequacy is from God (2 Corinthians 3:5 NAS).

At almost fifty-four years of age, I have reached the status of being an older woman who has seen more years in my past, than I anticipate in my future. Thirty-six years ago, when I met my high school sweetheart, my greatest dream in life was to marry and raise a bunch of kids. Now, as the mother of six, wonderful daughters, and grandmother of ten with two more on the way, I look back in amazement at the fulfillment of a childhood dream.

Over forty years ago, I accepted Jesus Christ as my personal Savior, and now it is impossible for me to imagine my life without Him. I can testify to His presence through both the good times and hard times in my life. He has *always* been faithful to me.

Often, I struggle in trying to articulate my thoughts, and feelings of inadequacy taunt me. Then I remember it is not my competence, but a competence found in the Lord that encourages me to press on. The Lord has etched His testimony on the pages of my life, and that testimony is what I desire to impart to you. As you journey with me through my pilgrimage of suffering, I pray that you might grasp the depth of the Father's love and compassion.

I raised you up for this very purpose, that I might display my power in you and that my name might be proclaimed in all the earth (Romans 9:17 NIV).

Introduction

I have a story to tell.

At times, I think, perhaps it is an autobiography, and then, I realize this story is not about me. At other times, I think it is about the well-lived life of my daughter, but that too, falls short. Is it a testimony—something that gives witness to a series of events? Is it a love story of God's unrelenting love, mercy, grace, and charity? Or, on the other hand, is it a saga involving a complicated series of events, personal experiences stretching over time; or is it a tragedy that evokes feelings of sorrow?

These questions I cannot answer, but I do know that this story is about a transcendent God who went before me and never left me; who carried me, comforted me, and raised me up with His story to tell. It is my hope that in the pages of this book, you will find hope and assurance.

Praise be to the God and Father of our Lord Jesus Christ, the Father of compassion and the God of all comfort who comforts us in all our troubles, so that we can comfort those in any trouble with the comfort we ourselves have received from God (2 Corinthians 1:3-4 NIV).

Within days of the accident, God impressed upon my heart a desire to write the story, **Kiss Goodbye**. God was clearly going ahead of me on this journey.

***

I remember the moment as clearly now, as when it happened then.

There she was—her slender five-foot eight body leaning back against the refrigerator, as she balanced on one leg. Her right foot tucked securely behind her left calf. Bare shoulders flattened against the door accentuating her taut tummy and tiny waist. Curved hips protruding slightly forward and slender arms relaxed at her side, as graceful piano fingers drummed lightly on her thighs. Her head turned slightly to the right and tilted upward, and her pretty face outlined by her short, honey blonde hair.

Her bright blue eyes twinkled as they followed me, as I scurried back and forth across the kitchen. She seemed to find enjoyment in watching me. A playful smile—perhaps even a hint of a smirk beamed from her face, as she appeared to be holding back a laugh.

I grabbed my purse off the counter and headed toward the front door. As I brushed past her, she reached out and stopped me. She spun me around until we were face to face. Wrapping her slender arms around me, she drew me into a huge hug that left no space between us and in a tender voice, she whispered into my ear, "I love you so much." Then loosening her grip, she stepped back ever so slightly before pressing her lips firmly against mine and gave me a momentous *Kiss Goodbye.*

Then I left.

I can remember ... *the light scent of her perfume—a hint of citrus, mixed with sweet flowers ... the feel of her silky hair as it brushed lightly across my face ... the taste of the sweetness from her lips ... the whisper of her endearing words ... her arms reaching out to me ....*

And to think I almost missed it! *I would have missed it. If she had not literally stopped me—I would have missed it.*

I had no way of knowing it would be her final Kiss Goodbye … unthinkable that I could have missed it.

But, I didn't—God ensured, that I did *not* miss that precious moment.

God did not send me into the dark night, empty handed, nor would He bring me through without something tangible to share.

Come now, as I share our story.

Our Family Then

Our once large household of eight had dwindled.

Mark, my husband of twenty-six years, worked for Marvin Windows and Doors as a human resource specialist.

I worked at Altru Medical Clinic as a receptionist.

Jennifer (twenty-five years old) along with her husband, Joe, and two-year-old daughter Ryan, had just moved to Texas. They were expecting their second child in ten weeks.

Laurie (twenty-three years old) had just graduated from college and lived in our hometown of Warroad with Rhody and two daughters Kaitlyn (six years old) and Savannah (four years old).

Catherine (almost twenty years old) had just graduated with her degree as a Practical Nurse and was preparing to take her Minnesota Board of Nursing exams to receive her nursing licensure.

Christy (eighteen years old) had graduated in May from high school and was excited about starting college and sharing housing with her sister, Cathy.

Keri (sixteen years old) would be a junior in high school in September.

Sarah (thirteen years old) would be an eighth grader in September.

The Moment of Truth

- the moment at which one's character, courage, skill, etc. is put to an extreme test; critical moment

—The Random House Dictionary
of the English Language
Random House, New York, New York

That moment of truth is indelibly etched in my mind as the moment life took an abrupt turn; the moment fortitude and desperation rivaled; the exact moment character, courage, and skill were put on trial; the critical moment, so extreme, I was forced into autopilot; the moment so raw and horrific, that nothing but the Grace of God would suffice.

Thursday, July 27, 2000

Perhaps Satan had asked to sift me as wheat.

*Simon, Simon, Satan has asked to sift you as wheat.
But I have prayed for you, Simon, that your faith
may not fail. And when you have turned back,
strengthen your brothers (Luke 22:31-32 NIV).*

It was a typical Thursday, a beautiful mid-summer Minnesota day, no different from any other day. Although I enjoyed my job as a receptionist, my family was of the utmost importance to me and I always looked forward to spending time with them.

My husband has always been a steady, dependable man, who has blessed me with his unconditional love. At this stage of life, I was content; I had enjoyed our past together, so full of precious memories, and waited with anticipation for our future.

I considered myself fortunate to be the mother of six beautiful daughters. They kept our life full of excitement, never allowing us time to be bored. It was an incredible experience to see them maturing into women of character, full of passion and life. Less than three months earlier, we had witnessed three of our daughters graduate—three weeks in a row. Cathy, our third child, had been the first to graduate, receiving her associate degree in practical nursing. I can still see her eyes shining with pride, as we presented her with a dozen pink long-stemmed roses at her pinning ceremony. The following week, Laurie, our second child, the mother of two little girls, had graduated with her four-year degree in business administration. As her parents, we knew what determination and fortitude it had taken her to accomplish that milestone and it was our pleasure to present her with a dozen yellow long-stemmed roses following her closing exercises. One week later, we had stood and clapped as Christy, our fourth child crossed the auditorium stage to receive her high school diploma and gold medallion signifying her honor student status. We celebrated her accomplishment with an open house following the ceremony. Roses were reserved for college graduations.

The three sisters were ready to embark on a weeklong excursion to Florida to celebrate their joint graduations. Cathy and Christy's suitcases were lying open beside their beds, as daily, they had been adding things. With their itinerary resolved, the count down had begun—only five days to go!

I had hurried home from work that day and quickly put together a spaghetti dinner, setting the table for four of us, Mark, Sarah, Cathy and myself, knowing Christy and Keri were working and would not be home to join us. Sarah still remembers that spaghetti dinner. It was the first and only time I ever added garden zucchini into the sauce. It was my attempt at using some of the bounty from Mark's garden and at the same time, adding a little extra nutrition.

As I cooked, I reflected back, amazed by how quickly the time had passed. Why, it felt like only yesterday I had come home from the hospital with Jenn, our firstborn, and now she was already twenty-five years old, a wife and a mother. And then to think that Sarah, my baby, was thirteen. I remember fearing those teenage years, but now I welcomed them. Over the years, we had dealt with our share of issues, but looking back it was easy to see how some things were just a phase. My own maturity had put things into perspective and most of the time I could see that —*this too would pass away*.

The three of us were seated around the kitchen table enjoying supper, when Cathy arrived home from her twelve-hour shift at the care center.

While writing this, I am taken back in time, and find myself remembering some of Cathy's traits. It was common for her to work a twelve-hour day. She loved being a nurse, and her unique passion for the elderly enabled her to relate to them in uncanny ways. She would often prance into the care center, dressed in her crisp white uniform, and ask the nurses if anyone wanted to go home. More often than not, there was an eager coworker happy for the time off and more than willing to take her up on the offer. A student at the time, the extra hours helped financially, but her deeper motivation was the opportunity to spend time with the residents. Her co-workers often teased her about how she pampered the residents. They knew how she would slip special perfumed lotions (a no-no) into her pocket and bring them to work. Then, while taking care of a resident's personal needs, she would add her own special touch by applying these lotions before helping them dress, always taking the extra time to add a little piece of jewelry, perhaps a little lipstick, or aftershave. It was important to her to do the extra little things that helped to maintain their dignity. She considered it an honor.

She had an infectious personality and was known for her playful antics, such as racing wheelchair-bound residents down the hallway and playing tag with others. With an outstretched hand, she would touch them as she whizzed past them calling out, "You're it!" leaving them waiting for the next time she passed by, when it became their turn to try to tag her back. Her exchanges with them created a sense of camaraderie, and her gifted touch affirmed their value.

Cathy promptly dished herself a plate of spaghetti and set it on the table. Glancing toward me, as she pulled out her chair, it was as though she could read my mind. She quickly excused herself and changed out of her white uniform before returning to the table. Before long, she began to share the finer points of her day with us. Cathy's love and respect for the residents, coupled with her gift for storytelling, beckoned our riveted attention. One of our favorite stories involved her interaction with an elderly patient suffering from Alzheimer's disease.

At home on a semester break from college, Cathy picked up a few available shifts at the care center. She had been gone for several months and looked forward to visiting with the residents. Arriving at work for a day shift, she checked the list of residents assigned to her care and was excited to see the name of a favorite resident. After report, she eagerly entered her room anticipating a warm response, but instead was disappointed and shocked when she realized the resident no longer recognized her. Feeling almost hurt, she began the morning grooming routine, helping her to wash and dress, all the time applying her personal touch before transporting her to the dining hall for breakfast. Throughout her twelve-hour shift, she continued to give one on one care, talking with her as she had done in the past. In the afternoon, Cathy had a little extra time and chose to spend it with her. She lovingly massaged a little lotion into her fragile skin, freshened up her lipstick and styled her hair. Pleased with the results, Cathy turned to put away her toiletries. Feeling a hard smack on her back, she quickly spun around making eye contact with the resident who proudly proclaimed, "You're it!" Cathy was thrilled, as she realized her personalized care had obviously spurred a memory for this dear one. This incident was indicative of the positive impact Cathy had on residents.

It was almost seven o'clock before we finished visiting around the table and began to clear the dishes. Conflicting schedules had stymied the frequency of family meals causing Mark and I to savor the times they were possible. *Mark—he was so proud of his girls. Some men wanted sons, not him. He was always quick to say he got the best—seven women to cater to his needs and he was not complaining!*

I mentioned to my family that I was going out to meet Mary, my close friend of almost fourteen years. Over the years, Mary and I had shared our greatest joys and personal disappointments and at times had provided a sounding board for the other. This was not really one of those times, rather just an evening together to catch up on each other's lives over a cup of coffee.

Just before I left, is when the momentous moment happened.

… the huge hug, the tenderly spoken words, and the final Kiss Goodbye …

… the moment she stopped me … the moment God ensured I did not miss … the moment I would remember and cherish forever … the moment that would become the inspiration for writing this book.

The Accident

I returned home just after 9:45 p.m., and rushed to the phone to dial my daughter Jenn. It had been one-whole-day since I had last talked to her and I dearly missed her. Our friendship had gone through a complete metamorphosis since she had entered motherhood. I could chuckle now we were such good friends, but I had not forgotten how easily she could exasperate me during her teen years.

It seemed longer than six days since I had kissed her goodbye, as she and her family had climbed into the moving van to begin their trek to Texas. It wasn't the first time she had moved away. She had been away at college and had lived several hours away during the first year of her marriage, but somehow that was different. Then, I knew I could hop in the car and drive to her. Now, with seventeen hundred miles between us, that was no longer an option. In addition, saying goodbye to our two-year-old granddaughter made it even harder. My consolation was that I would see them again in two months for the birth of their second daughter, a sister for Ryan and a fourth granddaughter for us. It was amusing that we had given birth to six daughters and thus far, those daughters had only produced granddaughters. Someday, I was sure, the boys would come, but I loved little girls and was thankful for the gift that each one was.

Anxious to hear Jenn's voice, I hurried to the living room to call. We hadn't been talking very long, when I heard the sound of sirens in the distance and minutes later noticed the flashing lights of the ambulance and police cars, as they raced past my living room windows. Sirens were always an eerie sound; they were never a sign of something good. They conjured up visions of tornadoes, fires, emergencies—*accidents*. My heart skipped a beat and a horrid thought flashed through my mind. I said to Jenn, "There must have been a bad accident—better not be one of my kids." We talked for a few more seconds, until I looked up and saw Mark coming down the hall—fear and anxiety written all over his face. I abruptly ended our conversation saying, "Dad is worried; I better go for now. I'll let you know if it is anything serious."

I got up, bracing myself as I walked those few steps to our front foyer. Mark and I entered at the same time and I remember the look he gave me as my right foot touched the carpet, a look that caused my stomach to drop. Then I heard him say—*three simple words—unforgettable words that pierced my heart.*

"Cathy—she's rollerblading."

My heart sank, as the same horrid thought flashed through my mind for a second time—*there must have been a bad accident—better not be one of my kids.* I crumbled. On the inside, I could hear myself screaming, "No, not my Cathy," but no sound was coming out.

In that split second, we both heard God say, *"The accident, it's Cathy—she's gone."*

My body shifted into autopilot. In a calm voice, I called downstairs to tell Sarah we were going out and would be back shortly. My voice was natural enough that Sarah would later tell me, she thought we were going out for ice cream or to the store. It certainly wasn't something that I controlled.

As Mark and I stepped outside and walked toward our car, I felt my body curl into an almost fetal position. My shoulders rolled forward as though protecting internal organs and my head hung low. Shock tempered my emotions. We climbed into our car and Mark drove to the end of our driveway and then stopped. He got out and returned a second later with *Christy's* shoes. Seeing them was like putting the final piece in a puzzle, clearly Cathy had worn Christy's shoes to the end of the gravel driveway before putting on her rollerblades. An unsettling wave of nausea swept over me and for the second time we heard God say:

"The accident, it's Cathy—she's gone."

Silently, we drove toward the flashing lights.

We had built our home seven years earlier, falling in love with the location. Only two miles outside of town, it was close enough to run back and forth to town, as needed. The gravel road into our development housed only three other homes, creating a neighborhood, yet still offering the privacy of country living. The connecting county road was a two-lane highway that provided access to town. Twice a day it generated thirty minutes of rush-hour traffic; the remainder of the time, it was safe enough to enjoy a leisurely stroll. Often, Mark and one or more of the girls would take a morning run along this road.

We could see down the road where all the emergency vehicles had converged less than half a mile away. Driving there seemed to take an eternity. Mark parked our car on the graveled shoulder and together, we began to walk in slow, robotic movement toward the scene, both of us utterly silent. Three emergency medical technicians watched as we approached—their faces were not welcoming. Still moving mechanically toward them, I heard myself speak in a voice that commanded their attention.

"The accident—it's a girl—she's wearing rollerblades —it's Cathy."

Their faces paled, and they were speechless. Wayne, who was one of them, finally broke the silence saying, "Deb, I didn't know."

I replied, "It's bad, isn't it?"

He nodded, "Very bad."

Crying, I answered, "She's gone, isn't she?"

With grave resignation in his voice, he said, "I'm so sorry."

That moment confirmed my worst fear. I turned to my grief-stricken husband and said, "Now we know where she is." The attendants thought I was referring to her physical body—we knew I meant Cathy was in heaven.

Writing about the accident makes it almost impossible not to relive that moment. I can still hear those words—short, choppy words bearing a message of doom and despair, yet at the same time, I am warmed by the remembrance of God's reassuring hope and tender care. God was interceding through His Holy Spirit by speaking truth into our hearts and minds and by surrounding us with the Body of Christ. Wayne was not only an EMT, but also a member of our church, and he was the one who informed our pastor and my friend, Mary, about the accident.

Until this point, we had been restricted from moving beyond the outer edge of the area, but in light of my statement, that had all changed. Now they escorted us into the inner circle.

The sun had finished setting and it was dark outside, but the flashing lights of the emergency vehicles illuminated the vicinity. My eyes systematically searched the area for Cathy's body. Seeing the closed doors of the ambulance, I assumed that I had found her. Visions of what lie beyond those doors flooded my mind. The moment seemed surreal, but I was not alone in my perception; even those in charge were having a difficult time grasping the veracity of my words.

Mary, the most levelheaded attendant at the time, asked if we could describe Cathy's clothing. Although I was unsure of the specific details, I told her she was most likely wearing shorts and a T-shirt, but she needed something more conclusive. Although, there was no doubt in either of our minds that Cathy was the casualty, we understood their need for positive identification. Mary left for a moment, returning with Cathy's watch—the one she had so proudly worn while taking vital signs of her patients. No verbal response was necessary; the look on our faces was telling.

The child I had named at birth, who had been lying nameless in the ditch, I now named for a second time. No longer was she merely the victim; she was once again Catherine Watson, dearly loved daughter of Mark and Deb, and beloved sister of Jennifer, Laurie, Christy, Keri, and Sarah.

Mark and I appeared to be handling everything quite well—managing with some level of coherency. However, our calm behavior was indicative of shock—shock that was sheltering us from reality—shock that was buffering our responses—shock that would be short-lived.

It took a while before either of us thought to ask someone for the details of the accident. Then Mark asked one of the state troopers, who in turn read us the statement that he had taken from a witness of the accident.

He (the witness) had been traveling south on the west side of the highway. He was going about fifty-three miles an hour and was just about to set his cruise control when a black truck came up behind him and began to move into the passing lane. About the same time, he (the witness) saw Cathy rollerblading north on the east side of the highway right near the white line next to the shoulder of the road. The next thing he heard was a thump and he knew she had been hit. He (the witness) put on his brakes and pulled over, got out and ran into the ditch. Finding her body about twenty feet away, he immediately felt her neck for a pulse and was unable to find one. He then felt her ribs to see if he could feel her breathing.

Although, I remember being there, as they communicated those details to us, I have no recollection of my response.

A few minutes later, I overheard Mark ask to see Cathy. The officer advised him against doing so, but plainly, nothing was going to deter Mark. Given little choice, the officer led Mark toward the ambulance, until an attendant stepped forward and redirected them to the ditch where her body remained unmoved. Clearly, we had arrived at the scene so quickly, that those in charge had not had sufficient time to process the details of the accident. Reluctantly, the officer took Mark partway down the ditch. At that point, I became vocal about my desire to see Cathy, as well. Almost grudgingly, another officer took me close to the edge of the ditch and shone his flashlight toward Cathy—my eyes followed the beam of light until at last I saw her—the perfect picture of peace, lying on her left side with her legs curled in a fetal position, in what looked like a handcrafted nest. Instinctively, I wanted to get close enough to touch her; but the officer was unbending in his resolve to shield me, going so far as to use his own body as a barricade. To this day, both Mark and I wish we had been more persistent. After all, this was our daughter, and it was our last chance to touch her warm body ever again.

A few months later, we saw pictures from the accident site. They revealed a startling truth. Her body had been anything but the perfect picture of peace; rather it was bloody, broken, and twisted—lying crumpled in a heap, like a carelessly discarded cloth doll—a body obviously devoid of a person; nonetheless, the body of our daughter.

When we regained our equilibrium, we asked law enforcement for information about the driver of the truck. Hearing them state his name for the first time, we realized that we not only knew of him, but he was a second cousin to our granddaughter. He was a young man in his late twenties, a mechanic at the local shop, and the father of a preschooler. We could only imagine the torment he was facing and wanting to ease his distress, we asked permission to speak to him. They informed us that he was no longer at the scene, but assured us they had a record of all the pertinent information. In our state of shock, we blindly accepted their explanation. Later, we discovered that he had not left the scene, but was detained by law enforcement a short distance down the road. Apparently, they assumed it would be inappropriate for us to have contact with him at that time.

Mary, the ambulance attendant, once again took charge. Although we didn't know her personally, we did recognize her from around town. She was a petite woman, probably in her mid-thirties, who always wore a pleasant smile on her face. Because of her kind disposition, it seemed only natural that we would accept her help in notifying the immediate members of our family. By God's grace, I was able to provide her with several of the necessary phone numbers.

The first call that Mary made for us was to our daughter Laurie's home and at my request, she asked to speak with Rhody. Laurie, Rhody, and Laurie's two young daughters lived in town four miles away. When Rhody came on the line, I took the phone and told him Cathy had been in a fatal accident. Then I asked him to bring Laurie and our granddaughters to our home. He promised he would bring them right away. Rhody was a good man—he was good to my daughter and granddaughters. That weekend, I gained a deeper love and respect for him, as he became our advocate, discerning and attending to our needs.

The next call Mary placed for us was to the Dairy Queen where our daughter Christy was employed. After verifying that they were still open, she offered to go and pick Christy up for us.

Daryl, one of local police officers at the scene, had a rapport with the youth in our community and because of that, he knew our daughter Keri personally. When he offered to find Keri and bring her home to us, we readily accepted his willingness.

Confronted with the reality our children would be arriving home very soon, we felt a sudden urge to leave the scene and be there for them. As well, we knew we needed to notify Jenn of the tragedy. My maternal instinct to protect and comfort my remaining children released me from the scene. Without that impulse, I am not sure I could have left Cathy behind.

Our family doctor, whom we loved and respected, happened to be the coroner on duty that night. I knew that at some point, I would need to know the extent of Cathy's injuries as well as the probable cause of death, but for the time being I was satisfied knowing he would be making those final assessments. Because we felt compelled to leave before he arrived at the scene, I left word that I wanted him to stop at our home when he had completed his examination.

With that final detail taken care of, we were ready to go home. Death was ruthless. In a relatively short span of time, it had inflicted an insurmountable toll on our lives. Death had no regard for those it left behind—*those we were about to face*.

In the process of being sifted as wheat, my faith would be radically tested.

I prayed it would not fail.

A Time to Tell

We stepped back into our home—a home that would never again be the same. One hour earlier, our lives had been normal, happy, looking forward to the future ....

At eight o'clock Cathy had serenaded her dad with a piano concert, as he gardened, and she had entertained her little sister by improvising familiar tunes on the piano.

Cathy was undoubtedly gifted! I remember when she was in high school and the choir director had requested students to help accompany during contests. Cathy often played the piano before and after class making her a prime candidate. The student's musical selection was foreign to Cathy, creating a nightly struggle for her at the piano. Not one to give up easily, Cathy persisted at sight-reading the music. Then the day came for the director to critique the student and Cathy labored through the piece. The director was disappointed with Cathy's performance and hastily accused her of not practicing. Cathy was hurt and embarrassed.

The next day at parent-teacher conferences, I met with the choir director and she shared her disappointment in Cathy's apparent lack of preparation. I asked her if she realized that Cathy could not read music. Shocked she replied, "But I've heard her play the piano on several occasions." Then I asked if she had ever seen her sight-read music? Realizing her faux pas, she apologized to me and wondered how she might rectify the situation with Cathy. I suggested that if she could give Cathy thirty minutes of her time and play the song through several times for her, the problem would probably be resolved. She agreed to try that and in a short time, Cathy was ready to accompany the student.

Now it was over, there would be no more piano concerts, no more stories, no more hugs, no more sweet whisperings of "I love you," no more momentous kisses … no more of many things.

At 21:44 p.m., the Roseau County Sheriff's Department Activity Log had recorded: *three miles south of Warroad rollerblader struck by pick-up—unable to do CPR.*

In that split second, our lives were permanently altered.

As we reentered our home, the first thing I did was call down the stairs to Sarah, asking her to come up—only this time my voice no longer masked the truth. Detecting the distress in my voice, Sarah rushed up the stairs and as she reached the top, she saw her dad hunched over on the piano bench looking completely defeated and immediately her eyes filled with tears. He reached out his arms and she climbed onto his lap, laying her head on his shoulder. I came and stood beside both of them and taking her hand between my hands, I told her Cathy had gone to be with the Lord. I watched helplessly as her face blanched from the news. I witnessed her childhood tersely end. She was a mere child, too young to grapple with the death of a sister. She had always been the one to plan our family events. Although only thirteen, she had a beautiful mature voice that was matched with a tender heart. She was full of life—always ready to serve. Now, when I felt she needed me the most, I had no choice but to walk away, leaving her wrapped in her father's arms, as I went to make my next call to Jenn.

By now, I was functioning by rote alone; my feelings were deeply repressed. I dialed Jenn's number, hoping that Joe would answer the phone, but Jenn answered in a drowsy voice and it was obvious she had been sleeping. I asked to speak with Joe for a minute. She became instantly frantic and began asking, "What's the matter, what's the matter, just tell me, tell me." I paused for a long time, and then told her. *"Cathy's dead."* She handed the phone to her husband. I feared the impact of the news on her vulnerable, seven-month, pregnant body. Joe took the phone and I repeated the news to him. He was shocked beyond words. Joe was like a son to us and we loved him as one of our own. His compassion and sensitivity had quickly earned our respect. Even now, I fully trusted him to care for my daughter, but I feared the stress might induce premature labor. I promised him I would stay on the phone with Jenn, while he found a coworker to come over in case they needed help with Ryan. He handed the phone back to Jenn and I told her the details of the accident. She was extremely quiet, but I kept talking to her until Joe returned home. Then I said goodbye, so I could continue making calls.

As I am writing, seven years have passed, and as I am revisiting that evening with each of the girls, I am discovering how horrific that night was for them. Sarah was the only daughter at home and the first we told. I thought she was safe in her father's arms when I left to call Jenn. I now know that within a few minutes she had left her father's side to call her best friend, but when she returned, her dad was preoccupied with the people who had begun to arrive. She was not comfortable in their midst, so she went outside and crawled into Cathy's car all alone. No one noticed she was missing and no one heard her cries—a mere child, only thirteen years old, unwittingly abandoned. Death had produced an orphan seeking shelter from the storm, but the only shelter she could find was the familiar interior of her sister's car, where she remained until her best friend discovered her.

After saying goodbye to Jenn, I returned to the living room shocked by the number of caring friends that had arrived. In a bewildered state, I sat down in the chair next to the phone. When it began to ring, I picked it up and quickly recognized the voice of Cathy's lifetime friend, Charity. Overwhelmed at the thought of relaying the news again on the phone, I simply asked her to come over.

In the meantime, Mary, and a second ambulance attendant had driven up to the take-out window at the Dairy Queen and asked to speak to Christy. At the sound of her name, Christy experienced a sinking feeling that only increased when they told her they needed to take her home. Although she begged to know what was wrong, at our request, they would not tell her. The two-mile ride seemed much longer as she silently battled the fear of the unknown. When they turned into our development, Christy saw the cars lining our driveway, heightening her sense of disaster.

Mark noticed their vehicle turn into our development and was on his way out to meet Christy, when Sarah, ravaged in her own pain, fled past him yelling to her, "Cathy is dead." With that affirmation, Christy collapsed on the concrete pad and let out a blood-curdling scream. Her dad lifted her into his arms and carried her into the house. As he attempted to set her down, she collapsed again, this time onto the living room carpet. By now, she was hyperventilating from crying so hard. Cathy and Christy were like twins, only seventeen months apart, best friends, and inseparable until Cathy left for college.

As the news spread rapidly throughout our community, more and more friends arrived to offer their support, and in turn, they witnessed our demise. Life had spun wildly out of control.

Our daughter, Laurie arrived next, with Rhody, and her children, Katie and Savannah. Laurie knew the truth. She had forced Rhody into telling her by refusing to get into the car until he did. He tried to get by with saying that Cathy had been in an accident, but she would not accept his ambiguity, and demanded to know the full truth. He had no choice but to tell her.

As Laurie climbed out of their car, she was greeted by the sound of Christy's heartbreaking cry. As the big sister, she felt a need to be strong—*to stay in control.* She came into the house and shifted into high gear. At only twenty-three years old, she was mature beyond her years. Immediately asking to use someone's cell phone, she called the airlines and booked tickets for Jenn, Joe, and Ryan for the next morning. Only later, in the privacy of her own home would she bear her pain; for now, she would remain a tower of strength.

Kaitlyn, our first grandchild, who was only six years old, had been watching her mom play Tetris on the computer, when Rhody had entered the room, calamity written all over his face. In a hushed voice, he had whispered to Laurie. Kaitlyn detected trouble and asked what was wrong, but they would not tell her. They would only say they were going to Grandma's house and she needed to get into the car. Angered by their silence, she got into the car without speaking another word until she saw me. The minute Rhody stopped the car, she jumped out and barreled up our front steps and through the front door. Her eyes keenly searched through the people, until she found me sitting on the living couch. She ran across the room and straight into my arms, begging me to tell her what was wrong. There was no point in sheltering her from the news, so I simply told her Cathy had died and took her to the window to show her the flashing lights from the vehicles that were still on the highway. Somehow, knowing the truth was easier for her to deal with than the secrecy.

Savannah, only four, joined us, oblivious to the ramifications of my words.

There were so many calls that still needed to be made, and as painful as that was, I knew they were my calls to make. Our bedroom was the only room not filled with people, so I went in there to call my parents. My mom answered the phone, and I was at a complete loss as to how to tell her, graciously, that her granddaughter was gone. Without giving specifics, I simply told her Cathy was gone—*in heaven*. My mom was sixty-eight years old, and it was very stressful for her to hear such tragic news, especially over the phone. She responded by asking me if she could come to Warroad, but before she could complete her sentence, she realized the absurdity of her request. Of course, she would come. She told my dad and he reacted by crying out, "No! No! No!" and running in circles around their living room. My mom had to grab him and force him to stop. The news had traumatized both of them. I was helpless; I had become the bearer of bad news. There was nothing more I could do than hang up the receiver. When my dad calmed down, he called the airlines to book their flights. The agent, who assisted him, was kind and did everything possible to accommodate their needs. My dad was seventy-eight years old, and I was thankful for the agent's compassion.

Charity had detected stress in my voice when she had called earlier and decided to head over right away. She had been staying at the home of her sister-in-law, Christie, and her nine-month-old niece. She told Christie she was going to our house and Christie decided to ride along. They lived a short distance from our home, and as soon as they turned onto the highway, they could see the flashing lights of the emergency vehicles. Charity drove quickly there and pulled over near the barricade, jumped out of her car, and fled into the midst of the emergency vehicles. The sight of the ambulance made her nearly hysterical. She ran directly to it and tried to open the back doors. The police pried her away, insisting that she leave the area. Given no choice, she returned to her car and continued on to our house. Although she had witnessed the obvious scene of an accident, she couldn't bring herself to face the truth. As she pulled into our driveway, Sarah, still very much dealing with shock herself, recognized Charity's car and ran out the door yelling, "Charity, your best friend is dead!" In that moment, all possible hope was shattered for Charity and the truth became a harsh reality.

Even though I was reeling from shock, my maternal instinct was to gather my children together, but even that I was helpless to do. I had to wait patiently for them to be brought to me, one at a time. Needing the reassurance of Jenn's voice, I called her a second time reminding her that soon we would be together. She, in turn, told me their bags were packed and they were ready to leave for the airport. Joe's coworker and his wife were with them and had helped them take care of the necessary arrangements at that end.

I dreaded making the next call on my list. Jered, Cathy's boyfriend for several years had called earlier and had been patiently waiting for Cathy to return his call. Thankfully, he was living with his parents and I hoped they were home to help him cope with the news. As I dialed his house, I wondered how he would deal with the fact that Cathy was never going to return his call. I questioned how he would find the strength to live without her. Cathy had loved him, and in her absence, I had a desire to love and protect him for her. I was greatly relieved when his mom answered the phone. I shared the devastating news with her, and as I did so, I added her pain to my own. Jered was standing next to her during our conversation and I could hear him pleading with her to tell him what was wrong. The harsh news was wreaking havoc in every life I valued. Death was without mercy.

Scott, our pastor for the past three years, had a loving, compassionate disposition. As soon as he received the call from Wayne, he came to our home. The horrendous devastation was obvious as he entered, and he began searching through the faces looking for members of our family. There were so many distraught people, it made it hard for him to find us. Finally, he spotted Mark kneeling on the floor next to me, as I sobbed uncontrollably. It was a pitiful sight.

Before long, many who had come to offer us their support began looking to Scott for strength. As a pastor, he must have felt as though he had entered a battlefield. Clearly, the needs were beyond his physical capacity—it was up to God to intercede.

After a while, I got up from the floor, went to Pastor Scott, and quoted a verse of Scripture that kept going through my mind. "I know whom I have believed and am convinced that He is able to guard that which I have entrusted to Him for that day." [1] He gave me the reference, as he looked it up in the Bible for me. It was my first awareness of God's presence, since returning home from the accident. In those words, I heard God whispering to me, and in my heart, I was convinced that Cathy was safely home with Him.

In the middle of the chaos, the phone continued to ring. This time, it was my older brother; my mom had called him with the news. Living fifteen hundred miles away, he felt helpless, but at the very least, wanted to assure us he was praying for us. I was overwhelmed at that point and unable to talk to him, so I said thank you and hung up the phone.

By this time, I had talked to each of the girls with the exception of Keri. It seemed like it was taking an eternity for Daryl to bring her home. I was worried that she was going to hear about the accident from someone else. She had just turned sixteen; Cathy had been her role model. I knew she was going to be shattered by the news. Then the phone rang and I answered it quickly. At last, it was Keri.

For a brief moment, I felt relieved. A*nd then, she began to blurt out that she was at the hospital—a friend told her Cathy was in a very serious accident. She had tried to call home but the phone was busy—another friend rushed her to the hospital at ninety miles an hour—when she got there she started to frantically search all over for her—but no one knew anything—they could only tell her Cathy had not been brought there.* She barely stopped to take a breath and then continued—*she thought they must have taken her to Grand Forks Hospital—she had tried to call us again—but the operator kept saying hang up and dial again—finally someone noticed her distress and came to help her place the call. They told her she needed to dial a nine first.*

Interrupting her flurry of words, I pleaded with her to come home, but it was as though she was deaf to my words. She just kept asking, "Where is she? Where is she?" Adamantly insisting, if they had taken Cathy to Grand Forks, her friend could take her there. Repeatedly, I pleaded with her *"just come home,"* but by now, she was frantic and unable to reason. There were no words of hope for me to offer. Reluctantly, I simply stated, "Keri, the coroner took her. Please come home." The somberness of my words finally broke through and I heard her cry out in anguish, tearing my heart even more. Her friend, who had rushed her to the hospital, had picked up enough of our conversation to realize what was wrong. He picked up the phone and told me he would bring her home. Powerless to offer any comfort, I hung up the receiver and waited for her to get here.

We later discovered that senior law enforcement had not allowed Daryl to leave the scene of the accident and in the intensity of the investigation, no one had thought to inform us of the change in plans.

Mark was still trying to reach his family, but before he could pick up the receiver to dial, it began to ring again. For the second time, it was my older brother wanting to make sure we were okay. I tried to tell him I couldn't talk, that Mark was trying to reach his parents, but in his own distress he was reluctant to let me go, so I simply disconnected the call and returned the phone to Mark.

At the scene, we had been asked if there was someone, they could call for us. Without hesitation, I thought of the Dieter family, who a year earlier had buried their nineteen-year-old daughter, Hannah, following a fatal car accident. At Hannah's funeral, I had witnessed their fervent faith and I knew I needed a Godly example to follow. When they arrived, I felt strengthened by their presence, and because of their own loss, they were able to touch our children in a way that others could not. Our children willingly accepted their open arms.

In due time, our family doctor, the acting coroner, arrived. I had requested that he come, but I could no longer remember why. Perhaps I had hoped he would tell me it was all a bad mistake, that Cathy wasn't really gone, that somehow she was okay. Instead, he looked at me sadly and told me the funeral director had taken her body. He shared his condolences with our family and assured us we could call him at anytime. Then he left.

At last, Keri arrived home. She slipped into the house, and like Pastor Scott, she could see the devastation. Her eyes searched carefully for family members. Her dad spotted her first and with tears streaming down his face, he rushed to her taking her into his arms and one by one, we joined the embrace. She was extremely upset and all I could think was this was not the way it was supposed to be. We wanted to be with her when she heard the news, so we could provide our support, but instead she was in the company of her teenage friends and although they were very kind to her, they couldn't take the place of her parents and siblings.

A sensitive friend, who had been busy helping in the chaos, came and led us into the kitchen to see the gift that Cathy had left behind. On the counter were freshly baked chocolate chip cookies sealed in baggies that were labeled with names—our names and the names of Cathy's coworkers. They were Cathy's last act of kindness and our first jewel.

I reflected on how Cathy was always doing nice things. Just this morning, when I opened the fridge, I found two sack lunches, one labeled MOM, the other DAD, and on the counter sat a beautiful floral arrangement she had given me two days earlier. I remembered her last words to me, "I love you so much" and then a kiss goodbye. On the counter sat the box of pancake mix and syrup she had bought for her birthday breakfast. Everything had been perfect. How could this be happening?

What had started out as just another summer evening had ended many hours later as a night we would never forget. It was 3:30 a.m. and our friends had just gone home. Laurie and Rhody had packed up their children and taken them home to their own beds. Sarah and her friend had gone down to bed. Mark, Christy, Keri, and I had climbed onto our bed and wrapped our arms around each other and I began to sob uncontrollably for the second time. After a while, Christy and Keri went down to bed, but rather than sleep alone, they chose to sleep together on the hide-a-bed.

Alone with each other, Mark and I began to wrestled with the raw reality—*our daughter was dead*. Clinging to each other, we fell into a restless sleep.

God Was Hovering

Our restless sleep only lasted a mere two hours that first night. As soon as Mark got up, he wanted to return to the scene of the accident. It was strange, as though something was drawing him there. I wanted to go with him, but the girls were sleeping, and I was afraid to leave them alone.

I poured myself a cup of coffee and wandered into the living room, feeling like a displaced person with nowhere to go. It had only been eight hours since the accident, but already the depth of loss was staggering. I was already exhausted from crying and at 6:15 a.m., the day had barely begun. Lack of sleep exacerbated my loneliness and it was inconceivable to think that my beautiful daughter was never coming home again.

In the midst of my sorrowing, the phone began to ring. I answered it quickly, not wanting it to wake the girls. Then I heard the sweet voice of a young woman we had known for years, the same young woman who had left our home only hours earlier. The intent of her call was so simple, to check to see how I was doing and if I wanted her to come and sit with me. She could not have known how lonely I felt and how much I welcomed her company. Now, years later, I still marvel at her courage and boldness—and sensitivity to the Lord.

A short time later, Sarah came upstairs crying. I wrapped my arms around her and wondered how I could console her when I was so broken myself. Then it was as though I heard God whispering these words to me, "I have loved you with an everlasting love," and I felt the warmth of His love flow through me and into Sarah. In that moment, I knew—*it was God's love I had to offer.*

When Mark reached the accident site, the first thing he noticed was the details of the accident mapped out on the highway in spray-paint. Later, we would learn that this procedure was forensic mapping and law enforcement used it as a visual aid in their investigation. Several branches of law enforcement had remained at the site overnight. Joe, a state trooper and family friend, was among them. When Joe saw Mark, he stepped away from the others to offer his condolences. After Mark talked with Joe for a few minutes, he realized the futility of being there, and shuffled home again. (As providence would have it, only two months later, we would stand with Joe and his wife, as they would grapple with the death of their sixteen-year-old daughter, Katie Jo).

I had been watching for Mark to return, and when I saw him walking up our driveway, I went out to meet him. He appeared to have aged overnight—he now had the posture of an old man. I wrapped one arm around his back and supported him as he labored to climb our front steps. I led him to the kitchen table, poured him a cup of coffee and set out the breakfast Cathy had picked out for him the day before.

It was only a matter of time before our home once again filled with people. A couple of the younger ones that came were Katie Jo (the state trooper's daughter) and our neighbor, Whitney. Two months later, we would remember their visit.

We had to open the garage door and set out lawn chairs to create more space for the visitors. Fortunately, my friends took command of my house, relieving me of the need to care for our guests. They even rearranged my cupboards to make room for all the food that people brought. Several times a day, a meal would be set out for our family and friends to eat and then as inconspicuously as it had been served, it would be cleared away until the next mealtime. The coffee pot was never empty and the lemonade was free flowing … only the hospitality came not from my hands, but from the hands of my dear friends.

Mark and I were concerned about Scott, the driver of the truck that had struck Cathy. Our hearts, though broken, remained compassionate, and we empathized with his situation. We wanted an opportunity to talk to him about the guilt we knew he would be dealing with. Later that morning, his boss brought him to our home, but Scott was so distraught he couldn't get out of the car. Mark and I went out to meet him and extended our forgiveness, leaving him with a hug.

That afternoon, when my youngest brother arrived we walked together to the scene of the accident. It was my first time back. Seeing debris from the truck scattered along the side of the road was shocking, and I gasped when I actually saw the mapping that Mark had described to me. The markings were descriptive enough that I could pinpoint where the truck and Cathy had collided and follow the pathway her body had taken before landing in the ditch. With no one to prevent us, we went down to the place we had last seen Cathy. The impression of her body, along with the stain of her blood, was still evident on the flattened grass and once again, I thought how much the area reminded me of a nest. We tried to comprehend what had happened. How it was even possible that our young, beautiful, full-of-life daughter was dead? We asked ourselves questions such as, "Why didn't she get out of the way?" and "Why didn't she see the truck?" We wondered if she had been scared, or if she had felt pain. We had so many unanswered questions that we would have to live with for the rest of our lives.

Overcome with anguish, we began to walk home again. Then, along the edge of the road, hidden in some tall grass, I noticed her rollerblade boot. I reached down and picked it up, drawing it close to my heart in an embrace. It was a broken boot with the wheels sheered off, but it seemed priceless. It was one of the last things to touch her body. Suddenly, I felt the color drain from my face and a wave of fear wash over me. My mind flashed back to the sight of her crumpled body lying in the ditch and I considered the possibility that her foot might still be in the boot. Mark seeing the trauma on my face, gently took the boot from me and felt inside—it was empty. In that moment, I began to grasp just how horrific the accident had been.

***

Looking back, I marvel at how things fell into place. The next morning, Laurie and Rhody took it upon themselves to drive the two and half hours to Grand Forks to pick up Jenn and her family from the airport. After leaving the airport, the five of them stopped at the house that Cathy and several other girls had been renting. It was a large two-story house with several bedrooms. A year earlier, Cathy had been so excited to move in with her friends and so proud to decorate her own little space.

Jenn and Laurie left the others waiting in the car and entered the house together, going directly upstairs to Cathy's bedroom. As they opened the door, they recognized her old navy blue and burgundy bedding from home. Then they noticed the posters tacked on the walls and the textbooks tidily stacked in the corner. Next, they saw the hand-painted daisies that embellished the freshly painted cupboard doors. The room was a reflection of Cathy.

Respectfully they entered, and began removing the posters from the wall. They felt as though they were violating her privacy as they rummaged through things to find her personal belongings to bring home. While searching through her drawers, they found her journals—journals that would allow us a bird's-eye view into her thoughts and dreams. When they were satisfied that they had gathered everything of immediate importance, they were ready to begin their journey back to Warroad.

***

Seventeen hours had passed since the accident, and finally, our fractured family was together —as together as it would ever be. After we finished embracing, I stepped back and looked intently at each one of my daughters, wishing I had a photographic memory. I had always *loved* them, but death had created a new awareness of how much I *valued* them. We were broken, but we were together.

God was hovering and someday He would reveal the beauty He would produce from these ashes.

Meeting with the Funeral Director

Jon, our funeral director, is a striking young man with a genuine love for God and a gentle, caring manner that puts you at ease, even during the most difficult times. His professional conduct and sensitivity creates an atmosphere of trust and respect. As a young father, he could readily identify with our loss. We felt blessed that he was the one to handle Cathy's body and make the necessary arrangements.

Jon and Pastor Scott came over, while Laurie and Rhody were en route to the airport. Jon had just begun to address some vital decisions that required our immediate attention when Christy, Keri, and Sarah joined us. Mark and I were comfortable with their participation. Jon anticipated the funeral would be well attended and suggested we use a larger facility than our home church. After some consideration, we settled on a sister church only a block away from our own church. Jon also recommended that we allow an extra day before the funeral to accommodate those who had to travel a long distance to get here.

After covering those details, Jon gently brought up the need for a closed casket. Instantly I was defensive and looking directly at him, I told him, that if our children wanted and needed to see Cathy's body, they could. Tactfully, he tried to discourage me from making that choice, but I was unyielding in my decision and retorted that if necessary, he had my permission to lay Cathy face down in the casket, but the girls *would be allowed* to see her. Jon, obviously distressed, asked if he could speak to me in another room. Standing in the doorway of the master bedroom, Jon said to me, "Deb, you don't understand," but before he could proceed any further, I assured him I did understand. I then said to him, "Jon, I don't know if she has a nose." He solemnly replied, "No nose."

I remained adamant that I wanted the girls to have the right to see their sister if they chose to, but we agreed that the viewing would be for immediate family only. Jon and I rejoined the family in the living room and decided to wait until the entire family was home before we planned the actual service.

Planning the Funeral

Jon and Pastor Scott returned the next morning to help us plan the service. Jon must have sensed we were more comfortable staying at home to make the plans, because he never raised the option of going to the funeral home. We had very little privacy with the continual flow of visitors, so we resorted to meeting downstairs in our unfinished basement.

Jon was sharing a few generalities about funerals, when Jenn suddenly recalled a pertinent conversation she had with Cathy about ten days earlier. Although she did not remember the context of their conversation, she clearly remembered Cathy stating, "If she died, she wanted to be buried as cheaply as possible, because she knew she wouldn't be in that casket." Cathy's own words became our lamppost in our decision-making. Rather than going to the funeral home to select a casket, we simply requested Jon to choose an inexpensive one on our behalf. Then, when faced with the dilemma of where to bury her remains, Cathy's own words again directed our decision and we chose the cemetery that did not require the added expense of a vault.

Keri produced the perfect picture of Cathy to use on the programs and looking at it, we agreed. Planning the service turned into a special time of remembering Cathy, and as a result, everything we chose was a reflection of her. As a family, God gave us a spirit of unity and the service came together easily. Mark intended to preach the message and each of us knew we wanted the opportunity to share our final goodbye.

Later that day, Mark and I went to the cemetery to choose the actual plot. That act was more than I could bear and I returned to our car leaving Mark to make the final decision with the ground's keeper. Once I was home, I retreated to the privacy of my room, locking the door behind me.

There was no way to escape the harsh reality of Cathy's death, but there was comfort in knowing that Cathy understood that to be absent from the body was to be present with the Lord. At times, I have wondered if Cathy had some premonition about dying. It seems unusual that a young girl would share her dying wishes and that she would have such distinct goodbyes for so many of us. The one thing I know for sure is that her death was not a surprise to God.

Cathy's First Birthday in Heaven

Cathy had been waiting with great anticipation of this day—the day she would kiss her teen years goodbye, forever. This day was to be her twentieth birthday.

Instead, the morning newspaper headlines read, "Warroad skater hit, killed: 19-year-old woman struck by pickup while inline skating on county road." We wondered how everything had changed so quickly.

We wanted to honor Cathy's birthday, but it was a struggle to know how to do that. Christy, the family baker, decided to make her sister a birthday cake. So right in the midst of the trauma, she baked and frosted a cake, determined that her sister's birthday would not be forgotten.

Jered came over to be with our family. Jered was never what I would consider tall in stature—but now, crushed by death, he too appeared aged and shrunken. At nineteen, he seemed too young to know such anguish. I wanted to ease his pain, but Cathy's death was final, and somehow, he, like the rest of us, would have to find a way to live with it. The best I could offer him was my support and shared tears. As he stood in our front foyer, he gave us the gifts he had bought and wrapped for Cathy's birthday. It was one more heart-wrenching moment; however, I will never forget what happened next. Reaching deeply into his pocket he pulled out a black velvet ring box and snapped it open to reveal a beautiful diamond engagement ring and wedding band. It was a purchase he had made that morning … a regret he tried to mollify. He asked our permission to have them placed on Cathy's left ring finger before we buried her. It was a bittersweet moment. We had looked forward to the day when he would ask for her hand in marriage, but this was not what we had imagined. It was a blessing to know how much he loved her, but it was bitter receiving those rings in her place. The obituary listed Jered as her fiancé and one of the ribbons that flowed from the casket spray read fiancée—but death had stolen their dreams.

Jered's parents were never far from his side, they were living with not only his pain, but their own as well. Cathy had lived with them during her first year of college and they had loved her as a daughter. Two and a half months earlier, they had stood beside us at her graduation, and with their new video camera, captured her as she proudly gave the benediction for the graduating class of 2000. We had expected Jered and Cathy to grow old together. We had expected to stand together at many special occasions. We had expected our families to be joined together for life. Now those expectations were shattered.

***

As family and friends, we once again retreated to the privacy of our basement, where we lit the candles on Cathy's cake—nineteen small candles circling the outside of the cake and one tall pink tapered candle in the center.

-Nineteen candles for her years on earth-
-and a single candle for her first birthday in heaven-

With tears streaming down our cheeks, we sang Happy Birthday, but we didn't feel happy. Mark and I had already bought and wrapped our birthday gifts for Cathy and several of her friends had brought special gifts they had intended to give to her. Sadly, I gave them to each of her sisters as a keepsake. The one exception was the wedding rings from Jered—those would go to the grave with her.

Weeping, I recited the latter part of the Twenty-Third Psalm from memory. *"Even though I walk through the valley of the shadow of death I will fear no evil, for You are with me. Your rod and Your staff they comfort me. You prepare a table before me in the presence of mine enemies. You anoint my head with oil; my cup overflows. Surely goodness and love will follow me all the days of my life, and I will dwell in the house of the Lord forever."*

As a mother, I was shattered, as were the dreams I had held for Cathy. I knew without a doubt, that only God could ease this loss.

The Keepsake Box

It was Saturday night. We were exhausted from the number of things we had addressed in that day alone—everything from planning a funeral, receiving a wedding ring, celebrating Cathy's would-be birthday, choosing a burial plot and welcoming our families.

Although we had received many visitors over the past two days, this night was different, because the visitors who came were Cathy's classmates from high school, those who had spent so much time with her over the years—those who knew her so well. Our living room suddenly felt full of life and energy; the weight of grief was lifted temporarily. Their presence was priceless. We connected with them differently, than we did with our family and friends; perhaps it was, because in their coming, they brought a part of Cathy with them.

The timing seemed right to bring up Cathy's keepsake box. Years ago, I had purchased six large Rubbermaid containers for storing the girls' mementos. With so many children, convenience was essential and although these containers were far more serviceable than fancy, they did the job. Whenever the girls brought home something special, I could easily pop up the lid and slide the treasure into the box. Over the years, the girls, too, began adding their own little tokens.

Now with her classmates seated around the container, I removed the lid to reveal the treasures hidden within. Carefully, I lifted out the first treasure, a nametag that was in the shape of a little girl and had the name Catherine Watson printed on the skirt. It took me back to her first day of school, when she had skipped out the door, so excited to be a part of the "big-girl world." Next, I removed the nameplate her teacher had fixed to her desktop in first grade and I wondered where the years had gone. Continuing to sift through the contents, we found awards and ribbons that reminded us of her accomplishments. Then, as she had grown older, she had obviously added things that were important to her, like notes from best friends, poems, and love letters. As we read the notes, her friends shed light on their significance.

Her friends spoke freely about her role as their spiritual mentor and the fact that she often carried a Bible with her. They told us about the time she stood up on the cheerleading bus and shared her personal testimony with the girls—telling them how they too could accept Jesus as their Savior. We felt comforted, as we embraced how much she *was loved* and how much she *had loved*.

That evening with those young friends was a balm to our souls, an unexpected gift. Indeed, Cathy's life had been short, but she had lived with zest and purpose. Now in her absence, her testimony challenged us to consider how we were living.

God Spoke to Me

It was late Saturday night—technically, Sunday morning. Unable to fall asleep, all I could think about was the accident. I didn't know how I could keep going. My precious child was dead. I was afraid to fall asleep. I was afraid to wake up and remember all over again. The house was quiet. I felt lonely. I kept thinking if only I would pinch myself, I would surely wake up and realize this was only a bad dream.

It is 3:30 a.m. and I am full of fear as I weep alone in the den. I feel a need to be strong for my daughters, but so many thoughts are pressing in on me. Sarah, she is only thirteen years old—I wonder how she will she cope? I can hear Christy's blood-curdling scream, as she heard the news. I cry out to the Lord reminding Him of these things and adding more to the list. Cathy and Christy were like twins. Keri is sweet sixteen, but it isn't sweet anymore. Laurie is so strong, but she has a breaking point. How will I release Jenn to go home again? My plea to God is a simple cry for help ... help to remember that He had not abandoned me, help to go on without Cathy, and help to hear His voice amongst all the anguish.

I pick up my Bible, turning it over, back and forth, not knowing where to turn. How can God fix this? He could have stopped it. He didn't. My Bible flips open and looking down, I begin to read.

Brothers, we do not want you to be ignorant about those who fall asleep, or to grieve like the rest of men, who have no hope. We believe that Jesus died and rose again and so we believe that God will bring with Jesus those who have fallen asleep in him (1Thessalonians 4:13-14 NIV).

I can't believe my eyes. I can hardly read as my tears cloud my vision. I know God is speaking to me ... He is acknowledging my grief. He is present. I feel strengthened. I feel His touch. He knows ... I am not all alone. He is right here with me.

I begin to think about the funeral and a message forms in my heart. I want everyone there to know—God is personal. Suddenly, I am excited, I want to wake everyone up and tell them what God has revealed to me. I feel at peace. I think I can go to sleep now.

"Oh God, how would I make it without You?"

A Breath of Normalcy

On Sunday morning, Mark and I woke up with a desire to go to church, so we dressed quietly and slipped out of the house before the others were up. It was a surprise for our brothers and sisters in the Lord to see us there. The service gave us the opportunity to share the very real presence of God in our lives these past few days and for that one hour, we were relieved of the burden of being strong for our children.

Later that afternoon, Rhody sensed our exhaustion from the continuous flow of people in our home and offered to take us out on the lake for a quiet boat ride. It was a welcome break and the afternoon proved to be not only a needed reprieve, but also an unexpected time of enjoyment, as Mark joined the girls and their friends waterskiing. For that short interval, our lives felt almost normal.

I believe that God orchestrated that time so we would be refreshed and better prepared to face the depth of what yet awaited us.

Preparing for the Viewing

It was now Monday morning, and the viewing was planned for that evening. The last time I had seen Cathy was Thursday night and even then, it had been dark. I wondered if I would be shocked—still I was anxious to see her. I was not concerned with how she looked— she was mine and I coveted this last chance to behold her earthly body. I knew she had departed from that body, but I needed to see her one last time.

I remember it like yesterday… *thinking, "Tonight, tonight my questions will be answered. At last I will see."*

Why would I tell you this? Why did I put myself through this? Would I not have been better to remember her the way she was? I can only tell you there was something sacred happening; something even I could not comprehend.

I remember being glad that we had reserved this night for us. We—her parents and her sisters—we needed the privacy. The girls—I did not think that they would accept that she was gone, unless they saw her for themselves.

Clearly, Jered had a need to see her, too, but I could not bear to see him suffering. His parents agreed to accompany him—I thought Catherine would understand. Poor Jered, he was crumbling. His world was falling apart. His dreams were shattering. He was in love with Cathy, and now their future was gone.

For days, Mark and I had not given any thought to our appearance, but in light of the funeral, that changed and we realized that we were both in need of a haircut. We knew the local beauty shop that had served us for years, was closed on Mondays, but we felt comfortable calling the owners at home and asking for their help. Graciously, they agreed to meet us at the salon. When it was time to pay for the services, we realized that in our troubled state, we had left our wallets at home. Compassionately, they told us not to worry, but to consider it a gift. Their benevolence deeply blessed us.

Then, before heading home, we stopped at the grocery store to pick up a few things. Because a thoughtful friend had opened a store account in our name and placed a large deposit on it, we did not have to be concerned with money. This practical gift was a great blessing to our family.

Arriving home, the girls met us at the door. Their faces were radiant and I wondered what had spurred their excitement. They asked us to sit down and listen as they read an excerpt from Cathy's journal. She had made the entry in her senior year, after returning from the funeral chapel where she had viewed the body of her friend Sam, who had died in a car accident. It read as follows:

Monday, Nov 3, 1997

Dear Sam,

I guess I haven't talked to you in a while, but I suppose now's as good a time as any. How've you been? We miss you already, and you've only been gone three days! Crazy huh. I'll never forget how crazy everyone went when you moved here in the sixth grade. I've never seen people argue so much over who got to sit by you at lunch. But no matter where you sat, someone was always upset that they were too far away or that there wasn't enough room at your table. But everyone got their turn. It's too bad you and Ole didn't work out. You would have been great together. We missed you in the band tonight. Jack was gone too, so we sounded pretty bad. The last one turned out all right, though. I was thinking about you and wishing you were there. Not everyone played, but you wouldn't believe how beautiful it sounded when you and the angels started to sing. I could hear you clearest of all. You always did stand out a bit. I know you had some bad times and went your separate way for a while, but I was really glad you decided to come back to school this year. We all were. Remember when we wrote our vows to never wear bell-bottoms and to always promise to remember each other when we were old and famous when we were in seventh grade? I still haven't worn them, you know; and I haven't forgotten you. Even though you're only eighteen, you're famous to me and I'm glad I got to spend the time I had with you. You'll have to give me a ring every once in a while to let me know how you're doing. Please say hi to Jenny and Jordan for us and make sure they are doing all right. Take care…hope to hear from you soon.

Love always,
Katrina Van Tassel
(Cathy's alias name from Spanish class)

P.S. They showed us some girl tonight and said it was you, but I knew it was a mistake. You don't need makeup to be beautiful, and I'm sure if it were really you, we'd have seen your familiar smile and a warm hello. I knew you were already gone, but I tried to be nice and said hi to the girl anyways. I'm sure you'd have done the same.

I was speechless, and found it hard to lay hold of what they had read to me. I felt guilty and wondered where I had been when she had faced this trauma. Why hadn't I known? Had I left her to face death alone? Questions, but she was not there to answer them. I read it again for myself, studying her handwriting. I was in awe of how she intrinsically knew things. I pondered her depth and was so proud of her. I only wished I could tell her. Then I wondered if Sam was with her now?

I marveled at how Cathy had grasped the truth about life and death and I was thankful for how God had been at work in her young life. Again, I sensed God's assurance, that He was truly in control and that He intimately cared for each one of us.

The Viewing

We went to the funeral home for the first time since Cathy's death. I have no recollection of how the girls got there. I only remember being in the car with Mark as he pulled into the parking lot. Most of my memory centers on my own experience.

I walked in. It was new to me. I had never been there before. I had gone to great lengths to coordinate all the details. I had promised Jon I would prepare the girls… I had tried.

I planned for each of us to have time alone with Cathy. Mark, as her father, would have his own time; he would not have to be strong for us. He could say his own goodbye. I feared for when he would see her. I didn't know what to expect.

We had agreed that Jon, our funeral director, would stay discreetly in the room. Mark would enter first and spend a few moments alone with Cathy before moving into the adjacent waiting room. Jon would continue to lead us in one at a time. I would provide support during the wait; Mark would offer support at the close.

We were huddled together in a small room behind the chapel. Jon came to share a few words with us before we proceeded. His eyes were gentle; he hesitated to speak. He asked us not to touch her body. I felt apprehensive; my mind was swirling. Doubts crept in.

Mark walked through the door. My heart twisted. I wanted to be there for him. What if—it was worse than I had imagined? What if—it had been a bad idea? Time warped; it rushed and stood still at the same time.

Apprehensive, I questioned the wisdom of my choice. What was I subjecting my family to? What had I done?

Without a sound, Jon came and led another through the door, closing it behind him. I fought the urge to press my ear against the door. I needed to remain calm, to stay in control. I was the parent; I could not let my fear show. The girls had already suffered so much.

Jon beckoned another to come. Again, the door closed. My imagination began playing tricks on me. I thought I heard crying; I felt trapped. I was needed; maybe I should scrap the plan. If only I had listened to Jon. Why had I been so adamant that the girls had a right to see? That door, it was separating two worlds. I was trapped on the wrong side.

The room emptied. Now there were more on the other side, than with me. Questions flooded my mind. How was Mark coping? Was everyone okay? …then it was my turn.

Jon is taking my hand; he is leading me. My legs are lead. Can I do this? I am looking into a satin-lined-casket; my daughter is peacefully lying there. Her hands are folded. The fingers on her right hand are bruised into the nail beds. A necklace is threaded through her fingers. I remember it was Jered's…he must have left it as a gift. Oh, the diamond ring, the wedding band—how they shimmer on her left hand. Although the left side of her body had sustained multiple injuries, her left hand appeared nearly untouched. She would have been so happy. Is she happy? My head turns slightly, my eyes travel up her body, her nursing uniform—it is familiar. Her nursing pins are proudly pinned on the white hooded jacket she is wearing. Am I breathing? Is this really happening? It is surreal. Time is suspended. I brace myself to look at her face. What am I seeing? Where is her mouth? Why is it covered with gauze?

I knew about her nose, but why can't I see her mouth, one last smile? I see one eye the other is bandaged. The cheek, it is her cheek. I recognize it—one small part of her remains. I love her. I want to touch her. Jon asked us not to, but I want to. Gently, I stroke her face. It is so cold. I love this body; this is her body. My baby, she is peaceful. She is at rest. I am not apprehensive. I am peaceful. God is with me.

How long have I been standing here? Have I stayed too long? I look to Jon. He is standing off to the side. He looks okay. He silently stands guard, like a sentinel in the room. I am thankful for him. He is so compassionate. I feel no pressure.

It is time to join the others…how do I let go and leave? Finally, I just walk away.

The others have been waiting for me. They want to go back in. They want to stay longer. We go together, and it is beautiful. We are all at peace. We are blessed to be ALL-together one last time. Together, we review our observations. We assess her injuries. We comprehend why Jon asked us not to touch. She is fragile. We innately understand that death was gracious, releasing her from confinement. Small tokens of our love surround her in the casket. We laugh and cry, and remember. We know this time at her side has been divinely sanctioned. God's presence fills our hearts. We are overwhelmed at His goodness. God has opened a window into what awaits us—our loved one is experiencing it.

We gather around for one last glimpse. Jon comes over to close the casket. The girls are ready, they turn one last time and say, "Bye girl."

Hope no longer flickers. It is radiant. We cling to it.

A Celebration of Life

Tuesday, August 1, 2000, was Cathy's funeral—the day that would have been the girls' flight to Florida. We exchanged the joy of seeing them off on their trip for the opportunity to share our Cathy with those who would attend the service. God provided an incredible empowering that day, as He allowed each of us to share our final goodbyes. It was not your usual funeral service. It was a service that opened with good morning and ended with good afternoon, a service that began at 10:00 am and finished at noon. A service attended by over six hundred guests, more than anticipated. It was a tribute to a well-lived life. To share it with you, I have to take myself back there.

It was time—time to say goodbye. As a family, we huddled together in the fellowship hall of the church. Strangely, I still remember the details of that morning, the clothes I was wearing, the place I was standing, and the thoughts that were looming in my mind. It wasn't our home church—our church was too small. Jon, our funeral director, had assembled us into a line for the processional. It was as though we were guests of honor at a special occasion, but the occasion was not coveted by any.

We proceeded to walk down the center aisle, conscious of the compassionate eyes following us. The sanctuary had filled with guests, and the side rooms had filled with the overflow. I was not feeling particularly sad, rather, I felt prepared for this moment. For several days, I had been planning the message I wanted to convey. My focus was not on the funeral, but the opportunity to share Cathy's commitment to the Lord, the reason for our hope.

Vicki, a friend of the family, was playing the piano softly and the music ministered to my soul. Our family filed into the front pews of the church, while Jim, Cathy's band instructor, provided special music. He chose selections that were uplifting and empowering and God used them to keep me focused on my purpose.

Mark opened the service by asking if Scott, the driver of the truck, was in the church. Someone pointed him out in a small room at the very back of the church. Mark stepped down from the pulpit and walked the length of the church to where Scott was standing, and then he drew him into his arms in a warm hug. People seemed to breathe a sigh of relief at the grace God allowed Mark to extend to Scott. A special tone had been set for the remainder of the service.

When Mark returned to the pulpit, he graciously thanked the community for their caring, compassion, love gifts and presence in our home over the past five days. We had received over five hundred people during those few days. Mark shared that our hearts are never physically closer than in a hug—creating a visual picture of our closeness together. Then he asked each person to hug the person next to him. He reminded everyone that we were not there to mourn the loss of a loved one, but rather to celebrate the life of a "live" one and that Jesus had given us a bright hope and a sure confidence. He then proceeded to sing "Jesus, the Very Thought of Thee" as Jenn accompanied him on the piano.

Pastor Scott prayed and recited John 14:1–6 from memory. "Do not let your hearts be troubled. Trust in God, trust also in me. In my Father's house are many rooms; if it were not so, I would have told you. I am going there to prepare a place for you. And if I go and prepare a place for you, I will come back and take you to be with me, that you also may be where I am. You know the way to the place where I am going. Thomas said to him, 'Lord, we don't know where you are going, so how can we know the way?' Jesus answered, 'I am the way, the truth and the life. No one comes to the Father except through me.' They were words of great hope and comfort. The congregation stood to sing, "Joyful, Joyful, We Adore Thee," one of Cathy's favorite hymns.

Cathy, with her friend Charity, had written the lyrics to a song titled "Stay Together" and Cathy had composed a piano accompaniment for it. Together, they performed it at their Baccalaureate Service, dedicating it to the Class of 1998 and the memory of their classmate Sam.

Two days earlier, while rummaging through Cathy's personal belongings, our girls came across a cassette tape with a recording of the accompaniment on it. The unveiling of this treasure now allowed Christy and Sarah to sing the duet, this time dedicating it to Cathy's memory. It was amazing, that not only did Cathy accompany the special music at her funeral, but she also spoke to those in attendance through the poignant lyrics of the song. God granted both girls the composure necessary to sing this touching piece.

Laurie approached the pulpit, bringing a friend for support to stand beside her. She, too, reminded everyone we were here to celebrate Cathy's life. She said Cathy had led a wonderful life, a complete life, a life that compared to no one else's she had ever known. She said that although Cathy wasn't with us physically, we felt her presence. Then she shared the privilege of going into Cathy's college housing to collect some of her memorabilia and finding Cathy's diary. Cathy could always make you laugh and was infamous for her daily lists of things to do, so Laurie read one of those lists from her diary. It included the simple reminder to "read at least one chapter of the Bible every day" and "pray before you shower—floss before bed." The simplicity of those words was comforting to us. Laurie highlighted that we knew where Cathy was and how much that was helping us. God granted her composure as well to speak the treasures in her heart. She closed by *saying that Cathy's impact was enough to provide us with a very strong presence of the Cathy we knew and loved.*

Jenn shared next, expressing her thankfulness for the extra time she had enjoyed with Cathy over the past four and a half months, while her husband had been away in the Border Patrol Academy. She told special stories that portrayed Cathy's unique relationship with the residents at the care center. She commented that as sisters, they had similar hearts and felt the same as Cathy, but no one had the ability to express it the way Cathy could. Her ability to relate to the elderly was matchless. Jenn proceeded to read an application that Cathy had submitted for a nursing scholarship. She pointed out it was not so much an application, as it was a picture of Cathy's heart. The essay spoke of Cathy's desire to serve as a nurse in long-term care and the rewards and satisfaction of knowing you could make a difference in the lives of the elderly. The final paragraph summed up Cathy's attitude: "Nursing, to me, is one of the most important fields there are, in regards to service. I feel that it finds people who are the most desperate and at the most difficult point in their life, and is able to turn them around so that they can continue on with their life. To be a part of that type of work makes me feel very proud, and I hope that I am able to contribute what I can to make that kind of difference." (A copy of the list from her diary as well as a copy of the application letter for the nursing scholarship is included in the coda of this book.)

Then it was my turn. I felt the eyes following me as I carefully walked up the steps. I began to speak, and my voice quivered. I reminded myself how much I wanted to do this. I put my shoulders back and stood a little taller, realizing God was giving me the strength and fortitude—I was going to be okay. Cathy's casket was directly in front of where I was speaking—a blue metal casket, not something of beauty, but plain…serviceable. I looked down at it, and I knew that she was not in it. She was in heaven, and in my heart, I praised God for that truth. I began by sharing the story of the accident and the journey on which God had taken us. My mouth felt full of cotton and some of my words got mixed up, but I wouldn't allow that to hinder me. I shared my conviction that you could not die a day before your time, and I challenged the guests, asking if they were ready—ready to meet their Maker. I told them Cathy had been ready and had accepted Jesus as her Savior and that fact was the basis for our hope. I also addressed Scott personally, assuring him God had control of Cathy's life, not he. He may have had the misfortune of being in the wrong place at the wrong time, but it was God alone, who held Cathy's life in His hands, and God who ordained her time to be born and her time to die. I returned to my seat as the congregation stood to sing the second hymn, "His Eye Is on the Sparrow," another favorite of Cathy's.

Then Keri approached the pulpit. I didn't think she was going to make it; she was a mess emotionally. Her friend had reminded her she was not doing this for everybody, she was doing it for Cathy. Clearly, that admonition strengthened her enough to allow her to speak calmly and articulately. She read a poem she had written about Cathy two days after her death. Accentuating her belief that God was in control, it captured her deep loss and grief. She humorously and graciously thanked the community for their thoughtfulness over these past few days. Then she shared the painful circumstances under which she had learned of Cathy's death. The details were wretched and a graphic reminder of the atrocity of death. No one would say death had come gently. She directed her final words to her sister, saying, "Cathy, I know you are listening today, and I wish I could tell you I love you one more time." She left the podium crying.

Christy, the daughter who had been so devastated the night of the accident, was now the one to bring laughter to our hearts. She opened by saying she wanted to "lighten it up in here a little" and read a paper Cathy had written entitled "The Art of Goofing Off." She moved on, sharing funny memories of growing up together, reminding us that Cathy had always had that one last joke. With great conviction, she said she thought Cathy was happy up there and was probably driving the angels crazy. The room resounded with laughter, and we sensed the people's hearts lightened by the assurance, we, as a family, would be all right. Christy admonished everyone to keep those smiles on their faces, and then she returned to her seat.

Sarah, so young, yet so confident, was the final sister to approach the platform. She shared that Cathy had always created special birthday cards for her and how she had been in the process of making one for Cathy before the accident. She remembered Cathy playing Ginny Owens' song, "If You Want Me To" before she left to rollerblade. She gave the context of the things she had written in the card and then read her card. She shared a few of Cathy's "would you rather" jokes, as I squirmed in my seat...in the end, everyone laughed at how humorous they were. Cathy had always been Sarah's champion in sports and Cathy had taught her the line dance she had been choreographing for the cheerleaders' Homecoming football game. Sarah shared her intention to finish it on her behalf. She closed by confirming her love for her sister and looking upward, she asked Cathy to put in a good word for her. The congregation laughed and then stood to sing "Amazing Grace" we were experiencing amazing grace.

Next, Mark sang, "He's a Big God" a song that spoke of forgiveness and dedicated it to Scott. Then he shared details of the prior weekend and the blessings God had provided. He said Cathy's life on earth was grace personified; that Cathy was a real prize, a real joy, that she loved to make stupid, goofy faces, that her warm accepting smile, that her passion, in particular for the elderly, and her peacemaking qualities had taught him much, and that we had a lot to learn from our kids. Jesus had helped him to understand how special we are to each other and had taught him to value youth. He shared that Rhody and Nick had taken us out on the lake over the weekend. He talked about waterskiing with the kids, and how they had deeply blessed him by accepting him as an old fogey, but a cool one. He then turned to the serious and preached a message of great hope, that included an invitation for all to receive Jesus Christ, personally.

Time had gotten away, so Mark suggested we skip the next song, but Pastor Scott said no, we needed to sing it.

Mark closed the service by singing, "Thy Will Be Done" — a song about accepting God's will in our lives—the choice we had made as a family. In my heart, I asked God to help me continue to accept His will for our lives.

Then the dreadful moment arrived—the time for the pallbearers to come forward and roll Cathy's casket out. I had remained composed throughout the service, but the finality of this act was unbearable. I stood, no longer tall, but rather hunched over in pain. I followed the casket out, my heart breaking and unabated tears streaming down my cheeks.

The Burial

We exited the church at the same time the pallbearers were lifting the casket into the hearse. Jon directed our family into a shiny black sedan. After he closed the doors, we began talking about the funeral amongst ourselves, expressing our thankfulness for the strength God had given us.

Then the hearse slowly pulled out in front of us and a hush settled in our car. Slowly, Jon pulled out behind the hearse. I turned and looked out the back window, noticing the long line of cars following us. I had never been at the head of a funeral procession before. Traffic was stopping to yield the right of way to us. We were moving at a snail's pace. I turned from looking behind me and my eyes latched onto the hearse in front. I was appalled at the thought that my daughter's body was actually in there.

We passed our church; the lot was filled with cars belonging to the women who were preparing the lunch to follow. We drove another couple of miles and passed our house. Our driveway was empty—for the first time in five days, no one was there. We were moving slowly and I could take in everything around me. I looked out the window to my left and I could see the road streaked with fluorescent paint. Then my eyes moved to the handcrafted nest in the ditch—the grass still flattened from where her body had lain.

The cemetery was ten miles out of town, but I was in no hurry to get there. The mood in the car remained tentative; each of us was fighting our own battle. The hearse turned right onto the neighboring county road. We were getting closer and closer—the time was drawing near. The hearse made the final turns before entering the cemetery road—a long narrow road lined by tall trees on both sides, that cut deeply into the woods. As we continued, I could see a clearing ahead and the wire fence surrounding the cemetery. The gates were already open, allowing the hearse access. Our vehicle pulled up to the fence and came to a stop. Jon opened the doors to let us out. Looking behind, there seemed to be no end to the cars weaving through the woods.

Jon led us through the gates toward Cathy's plot. This was only my second time ever being here. All of us were walking with our heads hanging down, with bodies that seemed to buckle under the load. The hearse pulled up behind the plot and the back doors opened. The pallbearers began to unload the casket and we watched as they carried it and set it over the previously dug grave. I had felt ready for the funeral, but I was not ready for this.

It was very still out, and I could hear the sniffles of my mom behind me. I had nothing to offer—my own grief consumed me. Once again, there was a definite hush and no one dared to speak. We had requested helium-filled balloons to release during the committal. Jon handed them to us and we turned and shared them with our families. Pastor Scott said a few words about the grave and our hope in heaven, and then he led out in prayer.

The time had come.

They began lowering my baby into the ground, and we let our balloons loose. She was being lowered deeper and deeper; the balloons were soaring higher and higher. Her body was being lowered into the earth to decay, the same body that I had carried within me, the body I had lovingly cared for, the body I had nurtured and loved. Inside I was dying—*my God, my God, why is this happening?* Only days earlier, we had been planning her future, now those plans were being lowered into the cold, damp earth with her. The sun was shining outside, but in me was a shroud of darkness.

In broken voices, we began to sing "Amazing Grace"—Cathy was amazing grace. The first shovel of dirt dropped onto her casket. I could not bear to watch any longer. I turned and walked away, trying to fathom how I could possibly go on without her. One by one, my family followed.

One Last Stop

We had one last undertaking before going home—one last stop to make.

We climbed back into the car and Jon drove us to our church. From the cars in the lot, we could see that a number of people had waited for our return. As we entered the building, a reverent hush swept over the room, and everyone turned to acknowledge our presence. It was now well past one o'clock. Someone led us to the food line. The women had prepared a gracious lunch, but my body was void of hunger.

We mingled with the guests, giving us an opportunity to show our appreciation to the many people who had taken the time to share their love. Then, we made decisions regarding the plants and floral arrangements that represented the love and care expressed by so many. With all the details taken care of, we were ready to return home.

Or were we?

Returning Home

I stepped into our home. It was finished. I had poured out everything in me to say my goodbye. God had sustained me. Now I was *tired … frail … wiped out*. What was I to do now? I had done everything physically possible to make the funeral a fitting tribute to her.

What now? What was I going to do? What was I supposed to do?

I felt like I was hanging from the edge of a cliff ….

Cathy was dead. What was I going to do?

Someone called to request a favor … could I look around the house for their cap? I told them I couldn't do it. Someone else called, thinking they had dropped something on the driveway … could I check for them. I told them as well that I couldn't do it. What were they thinking? Had they forgotten I had just buried my daughter—my nineteen-year-old daughter?

Our house was empty. What was I going to do? How could I keep going? I called out to God. I only heard silence. I longed to sense His presence. I didn't.

I was empty.

Through the Night

"When tragedy makes its unwelcome appearance and we are deaf to everything but the shriek of our own agony, when courage flies out the window and the world seems to be a hostile, menacing place, it is the hour of our own Gethsemane. No word, however sincere, offers any comfort or consolation. The night is bad. Our minds are numb, our hearts vacant, our nerves shattered. How will we make it through the night? The God of our lonely journey is silent.

And yet it may happen in these, the most desperate trials of our human existence, that beyond any rational explanation, we may feel a nail scarred hand clutching ours. We are able, as Etty Hillesun, the Dutch Jewess who died in Auschwitz in 1943, wrote, 'to safeguard that little piece of God in ourselves'[2] and not give way to despair. We make it through the night and darkness gives way to the light of morning. The tragedy radically alters the direction of our lives, but in our vulnerability and defenselessness we experience the power of Jesus in His present risenness."[3]

The Journey

The night was bad and there would be much more night yet to experience. The crucible readied—the refining fire stoked, there would be no possible way to make it through unscarred. It would be critical to remember the scars Jesus bore on His body—for I would not be spared. The God, who could have spared Cathy's life, had chosen not to. Would I, as Etty, be able to safeguard that little piece of God in me and not give in to despair? Would I be able to withstand the radical testing of my faith? It would be a long journey before the night would give way to the light of the morning. Many tears would fall along the way. The outcome remained uncertain.

The testing came quickly and relentlessly. The challenges were never ending. Each day produced new hurdles. Anticipation of the "firsts" created a sense of apprehension. Cathy's first birthday in heaven, our first birthdays, the first birth, first Thanksgiving, first Christmas, first New Year's, first life-threatening illness, first dream, first Easter, first Mother's Day, first Father's Day, first anniversary of her death—each yielded a broad range of emotions.

Now, years later, I ask myself, if these firsts were significant. Do they warrant discussion—if so, will it amount to more than mere verbiage? Yes, they are certainly more than verbiage; in fact, these firsts were the very threads that would, one day, unveil an unseen tapestry. In the meantime, God would use them to challenge my preconceived ideas. These firsts would be instrumental in bringing me to the place where I would embrace God as He is, not as I had perceived Him to be.

Plans for a Road Trip

As I have shared previously, when Jenn and Joe received the tragic news, they immediately flew home. Less than a week earlier, Joe had returned to Minnesota from the Border Patrol Academy in South Carolina to pack up his family and move clear across the country to Texas. The accident occurred after only one day of employment at his new station. His employer, though gracious in granting a leave of absence, required that he return to work the day following the funeral. Joe was reluctant to leave without his family. They had already experienced a lengthy separation.

As Joe and I discussed the need for Jenn and Ryan to stay behind a few more days, I felt his uneasiness and promised that we would send his family home soon. The unexpectedness of Cathy's death had created insecurities in each of us. Jenn was seven months pregnant and I was fearful of the effect this was having on her. I was trying to be sensitive to Joe's needs, Jenn's needs, and my own needs. The thought of sending them off, alone on a plane, was unbearable. Feeling in a quandary for how to address these needs, I suggested to Mark that it might be best to drive Jenn and Ryan home. Although the trip would entail almost thirty-five hundred miles, he wholeheartedly agreed and once the girls caught wind of our discussion, they wanted to come too. With this issue settled, we proceeded to make plans.

The first obstacle we faced was our vehicle. It was not big enough to accommodate seven passengers, plus luggage. Since we live in a small community that does not have a rental car business, our options were limited. Mark went to his employer and asked if he could borrow one of the company vans. They graciously lent us a brand new twelve-passenger van to make the trip.

The next conflict was Laurie's work schedule that made it impossible for her to travel with us. Although we were disappointed and did not want to leave her behind, we agreed to maintain close contact throughout the duration of our trek across the country.

Our extended family and friends tried to discourage us from taking such a major trip so soon after the funeral. They feared it would be too taxing, on us so soon after such a traumatic time. We acknowledged their concern, but felt the road trip was our best alternative for getting Jenn home again.

After some deliberation, we made plans to leave three days after the funeral.

Looking back, I clearly see God was going before us and meeting all our needs through people and the everyday circumstances of our lives. Things that seemed insurmountable to us proved to be simple for God. I am eternally grateful for God's faithfulness and the faithfulness of His people in our lives.

On the Road

Death had stirred much unrest in our lives, and as a father, Mark was no longer prepared to leave important questions unanswered. Although we were in the van ready to leave, Mark insisted that each of his daughters share with him when they had personally received Jesus Christ as their Savior. Because he knew that Laurie would not be travelling with us, he made a point of speaking with her beforehand.

It was Friday afternoon. Death had eliminated the restraints of time. Pressure no longer dictated our lives. We drove only two short miles and stopped at a local restaurant to share a farewell meal with Laurie and my parents. After savoring our time together, we said our goodbyes and set out on our journey.

Tired, and in need of a good night's rest, we drove a mere two hundred miles before checking into a hotel for the night. Rejuvenated, we hit the road early the next morning. We drove mile after mile, often unaware of what state we were passing through. We were listening to the Christian music Jenn's friend had lent us, and in doing so, we sensed God bathing our souls with the message from the lyrics. The aftermath of the trauma of Cathy's death had created a distinct change in each of us. The constraints of time no longer mattered, leaving us free to journey at our pace.

We called Laurie frequently, throughout the day, to stay in touch. In our conversations, we would update her on our whereabouts and our thoughts. Daily, she would pick up our mail and sort through it, collect all the sympathy cards and then share them with us at that time, as well as any other news from home.

We were nearing the outskirts of Oklahoma City as evening approached and decided to stop for the night. Entering the city limits, we noticed that traffic seemed backed up and hotel after hotel flashed their "No Vacancy" signs. It was apparent some significant event was taking place in the city. We continued driving toward the city center hoping to find lodging for the night. Our travels took us past the Concert Hall—obviously the source of the congestion. We saw long lines of people and then the flashing lights of the marquee, announcing "The Dixie Chicks in Concert." Within seconds, we were all in tears. The last picture taken of Cathy was two weeks earlier before she went to

"The Dixie Chicks Concert." Here they were, still on tour, yet her life was over.

Heartbroken, we gave up our search for lodging and set out on the road again. Mark was still driving when the first hint of daylight was visible on the horizon. He was exhausted and falling asleep at the wheel, when the van caught the shoulder of the road and began to swerve. I begged him to stop. We had already experienced enough tragedy in our lives.

He pulled into the parking lot of the nearest hotel and I went into the lobby. The clock on the wall read 4:00 a.m. as I rang the bell to summon the desk clerk. Sleepily, he told me he only had one vacancy with a five-person capacity. I told him there were seven in our party, and then my tears began to flow as I shared our story, beginning with Cathy's death and ending with almost driving off the road. Feeling sorry for us, he allowed us to stay in the room. Thankfully, the room had a king-size bed and a pull out sleeper and each of us to found a spot to stretch out on. Before long, we were all sleeping soundly.

I woke up several hours later, and went to the hotel lobby for a cup of coffee. I was surprised to see a large number of people milling around, with more arriving all the time. Curious to know why, I looked around and noticed the hotel letter board indicating a Church Worship Service in one of the conference rooms. I had lost track of time and was surprised to realize it was actually Sunday morning. Even though I hadn't been thinking about going to church, I was in awe of the thought that God had brought a church to me.

Moments later, a kind man introduced himself and invited me to join their service. I thanked him for his thoughtfulness, but said I had family waiting for me in our room. In a friendly manner, he asked what had brought us to Fort Worth, Texas. Once again, our story spilled out. He asked me to wait for a moment, as he motioned a small group of people to come over. He repeated our story to them and they formed a small circle around me and began to pray for healing in our lives and travelling mercies. Although I was miles away from home, God had provided the Body of Christ to comfort me in my loss. It was easy to see that God was not limited. In my heart, I worshipped.

We continued to drive throughout the rest of the day, finally arriving in Eagle Pass, Texas, in time for a late supper and early bedtime. Joe was happy to see his small family and I was happy to see my daughter's new home.

How I wished I could see Cathy's new home too.

A Time to Leave

The days in Eagle Pass flew by rapidly and before long, it was time for us to journey north again. I was apprehensive at the thought of leaving Jenn, as well as our precious granddaughter, Ryan. Jenn seemed so emotionally fragile and it was hard to leave her without any friends or church family. I kept replaying Cathy's last kiss goodbye over in my mind and I was terrified to say another goodbye. I pleaded with God to help me, not knowing how I could pull myself away.

Our last moments together were tearful and we clutched one another in despair. Joe stopped by on his lunch break to say goodbye to us and to console Jenn. When we couldn't delay any longer, I reluctantly climbed into the van. Through the window, I watched Jenn crumble into her husband's arms. Now, every few hours, I made two phone calls—one to the north and one to the south. How I desperately longed to make one vertical call.

Journeying Home Again

The journey home was much quieter; five seemed so much less than seven. The thought of returning home left me feeling uneasy. So many memories awaited us there, so many memories, so fresh, so painful—so many things yet to face.

As we pulled into our driveway, Laurie's welcoming smile greeted us. Anticipating our return, she had re-opened our home for us. Her presence was a solace. My heart filled with gratitude for her life, and holding her in my arms relieved some of the anguish of leaving Jenn and her family behind. In the past two weeks, my appreciation for my children had grown immensely. Never again would I take them for granted.

Together, we walked through the front door of our home. It was as though we were choosing to walk back into our lives—lives that were familiar, yet harrowingly different. It was yet another step on the journey through the night. The light of the morning was cast so far in the distance, that it remained unseen.

Laurie asked us to close our eyes as she led us into what had been Cathy's room. Cathy's scent permeated from everything. Together we sat on the side of her bed and inhaled deeply as though to drink in the aroma of her presence. We will never know what drew out her scent in such a profoundly perceptible way, but it was a fragrant gift from God—a sweet reminder of Cathy and reassurance of His presence in our lives.

A Dark, Distressing Night

We had only been home a few days, when Christy went to spend the night at a friend's cabin. The cabin was located on an island across the lake and was accessible only by boat. Christy called home late that night, sobbing and nearing her breaking point. At the sound of her distraught voice, anxiety threatened to take me down. I wanted to be there to console her—to comfort her in her grief, but the hour of the night and the remoteness of the cabin made that impossible. Mark's elevated stress level was causing chest pains and I knew I couldn't burden him further with my concern. Keri and Sarah were sleeping soundly. With nowhere left to turn, I cried out to the Lord. My heart was breaking.

Years earlier, I had suffered from panic attacks. Now with all the stress in my life, I feared their return. My anxiety escalated and fear consumed me. I gave in and took some anti-anxiety medication, but my already hypersensitive body responded negatively and I felt nearer to panic than before.

Again, I cried out to the Lord. He felt far away and I felt alone. Then I remembered my friend, Mary, telling me if I needed her, I could call her at any time. Desperate, I called her at two o'clock in the morning. She arrived within ten minutes and stayed for the remainder of the night. Her presence allayed my fears and lessened my anxiety. God used Mary's arms to be the arms of Jesus to me. A friend loves at all times … how blessed I was to have such a friend.

God Made a Way in the Darkness

Jenn's new home was in a predominantly Spanish speaking community. In the six weeks since she moved there, she still had not encountered anyone who spoke English. She seemed more and more despondent as she neared the end of her pregnancy. She still had not found anyone to watch Ryan, when she went into labor. Feeling helpless, I searched the internet for an English-speaking church in her community. Although she lived in a community of over thirty thousand, I found only two possibilities. I placed a long distance call to the first one listed. After several rings, a woman who spoke English fluently, answered the phone. In the course of my asking her several questions regarding the church, she volunteered that they were currently without a pastor. At that moment, the only thing that mattered to me was that I had found someone who spoke English. She graciously listened as I poured out my heart, and she in return, offered to go to visit Jenn. I was relieved that there was finally someone willing to reach out to Jenn with friendship.

Mark was also concerned over Jenn's emotional state and suggested that I go for a visit. I talked it over with Jenn and Joe and they were both excited to have me come. We quickly made the travel arrangements and I began to pack.

Up to this point, Joe had to work Sundays and Jenn hadn't felt up to going to a new church alone. My visit spanned over two Sundays, so Jenn, Ryan and I went to church together. The interim pastor was a warm, African-American man who heartily welcomed us as we entered the church. After introducing Jenn and myself to him, I told him about our recent loss, which he took the liberty of sharing with the congregation during the prayer time. At the close of the service, several people gathered around us to express their sympathy and to offer their support. I also had the chance to meet the woman I had previously spoken to on the phone.

God had made a way in the darkness and provided a body of believers to care for Jenn in my absence.

Surprise Gifts and Painful Reminders

As the months passed from one to another, many hidden gifts were unearthed and many painful reminders surfaced.

Jenn was an accomplished pianist and loved to sit at her electric piano and play for personal enjoyment. One day, as she was playing, she noticed a button labeled "record and playback." Without thinking, she pressed it, and much to her surprise, she began to hear the accompaniment to "Bare Necessities" from The Jungle Book. Ryan, hearing the tune, started dancing in circles, mimicking the special dance she had so often performed for Auntie Cathy. Without Jenn's knowledge, Cathy had recorded the arrangement on her piano. It was such an unexpected surprise and Ryan reveled in the opportunity to dance to her Auntie's accompaniment. Sadly, the joy was fleeting, because a short time later, Ryan erased the recording while trying to press play.

A related surprise was the discovery of a picture of Cathy playing the piano and Ryan dancing. It was one of those first shots on a disposable camera that acts as a tester—a negative that had never been developed. It was quickly developed, enlarged and distributed to everyone.

One of the most cherished surprise gifts was the sound of Cathy's voice. Upon returning home from our trip to Texas, I went to review the messages on the answering machine that was just recently set up on our computer. I was taken aback to see a flashing message from Cathy. Could she still be alive? The crazy thought left my mind as quickly as it had entered. I was so concerned about preserving the content of the message, I wouldn't let anyone touch the computer until I had a computer tech come and burn a copy of the message onto a disc. The machine must have picked up right as Cathy had answered Jered's call and recorded their two-minute conversation. While the content of the conversation was of no consequence, the simple exchange of words was priceless. I listened to it over and over and made copies for everyone.

Along with the wonderful surprises that God gave us after Cathy's death, there were, of course, some harsh realities as well. Credit card companies are not respecters of the death of a loved one. After the funeral, Laurie contacted all of Cathy's accounts to close them. One particular credit card company refused to speak to Laurie, stating that she was not the cardholder. She tried to explain nicely that it would be quite difficult to speak to the cardholder, who was no longer alive, and that she was taking care of closing her accounts. They ignored her explanation and continued insisting that she wasn't the cardholder and was not authorized to make changes to the account. We sent in the death certificate as soon as we received it about eight weeks later, but continued to get harassing phone calls. Finally, I had reached the end of my rope. When the credit company representative called to collect on the unpaid balance, I asked them, "WHAT PART OF DEAD DON'T YOU UNDERSTAND!" I told them Cathy had died, we had informed them this was the case, and had sent them her death certificate. If they called me again, they would be hearing from my lawyer. I am happy to say this was an isolated experience.

A Way to Remember

With Jenn living so far away, she was never far from my thoughts. God had placed her in unique circumstances that left her in the position of walking through her grief alone without the camaraderie of sisters or the companionship of friends. Joe was a wonderful husband, but his new job caused him to be gone from home for many hours at a time, leaving Jenn alone with only the company of a two year old.

Scrapbooking was the newest trend in preserving memories, so I thought that it might help Jenn to fill her days. Before flying out to see her, I scoured the local craft stores to find just the right assortment of papers, tools, and albums. Packing everything into my suitcase, I looked forward to Jenn's reaction. I was encouraged by her interest and it revived my hope that perhaps one day we would once again find enjoyment in the simple pleasures of life.

Not only had I packed scrapbooking supplies for Jenn, but also for myself. As mother and daughter, we spent several hours every day sitting at opposite ends of her dining room table sorting through pictures of our daughters—Jenn sorting Ryan's picture, me sorting Cathy's pictures. Scrapbooking opened the door for us to preserve our memories, as well as to provide a productive way for us to share our pain through the common bond of motherhood.

When I returned home ten days later, I was content in the knowledge that Jenn now had a new hobby that would keep her busy for many hours. I, too, had hours of work set out for myself. While I was at Jenn's, I realized what a blessing it would be for each of us to have a copy of a creative memory album of Cathy. With Christmas just a few months away, I set out to complete the task. I knew with certainty this would be a treasured gift.

God impressed the following verses upon my heart and it seemed fitting to have them inscribed on the final page of the album.

The good men perish; the godly die before their time, no one seems to realize that God is taking them away from evil days ahead. For the godly who die shall rest in peace (Isaiah 57:1-2NIV).

Welcoming New Life

I had been home from Texas for two weeks, when Jenn called home in an obviously grief-stricken state. The loss of her little sister was taking its toll. It was her birthday and her baby was due in two weeks. Events that would normally bring joy were instead, overshadowed by intense sadness. I had already purchased my flights to return in two more weeks for the delivery of her baby and found myself once again counting down the days until I would see her again. Her grief was so debilitating, that I feared for her well-being.

The very next day Jenn called to tell me she was in labor. My spirits plunged to new depths. I had planned to be there to care for Ryan. To make matters worse, Mark was out of town and I could not lean on him for moral support. I rescheduled my flight for the following morning and repacked my bags between updates on her progress.

Things seemed to spiral downward rapidly. The woman from the church who had agreed to take care of Ryan in my absence was unavailable, which forced Jenn and Joe to leave Ryan with their landlord. When they arrived at the hospital, the initial assessment raised concern and resulted in the doctor ordering an ultrasound. It indicated that the baby was in an awkward position, which would prevent a natural delivery and necessitate a caesarian section.

Alone at home, negative thoughts began to flood my mind. It seemed like an eternity between updates. Finally, Joe called to announce the birth of a healthy daughter, Reese Catherine, named in memory of her auntie. I knew, then, what it meant to be both sorrowing and rejoicing.

Reese had missed her mom's birthday by one day, being born instead on her dad's birthday. God knew we could all use a little cheering up.

A Third Trip to Eagle Pass

In keeping with this downhill spiral, Mark missed his flight home and I had to leave without being able to say goodbye to him in person. I drove through the night to the airport. Before boarding my plane, I used a payphone to call long distance to the hospital to see how the new family was doing. Jenn answered the phone sobbing uncontrollably. Again my spirits plunged. Hospital policy would not allow children to visit and this meant Joe wouldn't be able to either, as he was taking care of Ryan. I hung up the phone and called the hospital back requesting to speak with the hospital administrator. I gave him a shortened version of our recent experience and pleaded with him to make an exception in this case. After hearing how much Jenn had already endured, he agreed to allow Ryan to visit with Joe.

I flew most of the day before arriving in San Antonio. As I entered the baggage area, I saw a young couple holding up a sign with my name on it. Joe had arranged for them to pick me up and take me the remaining hundred and fifty miles to Eagle Pass. I was very thankful for their generosity. Three hours later, they dropped me off at the hospital to meet my newest granddaughter, Reese Catherine.

As I came down the hospital corridor, I could hear Jenn crying. My heart sunk in my chest and I wondered what more we would have to endure. The doctor was in the room with her trying to diagnose the cause of her intense pain. He ordered a diagnostic ultrasound and my imagination ran wild until he returned with the results. Gallstones … painful, but not life threatening. In time, she would require surgery, but for now, he would treat the symptoms.

Welcoming new life was wonderful, but the event had been shrouded in fear. I wondered if this would be indicative of our future.

The Bride Has Met the Bridegroom

Cathy loved fairytales. She especially loved the story of Snow White and the Seven Dwarfs and was enamored with the thought of someday meeting her prince. Now that her relationship with Jered had become more serious, she had begun to visualize her own wedding day. She had clipped and saved pictures of her favorite gowns, bouquets, cakes and invitations. A special memory of having her home for the summer was the hours we spent talking and elaborating on the finer points of a dream wedding.

One day, shortly after her death, I was lying prostrate on the living room carpet weeping, what seemed like buckets of tears. In my despair, I asked the Lord, why she couldn't have been a bride, even if she had to die later. Why couldn't she have enjoyed this one dream in her life?

Eventually I got up and moved to the couch. I picked up my Bible and for a second time, split it open. The very first words I read were, "The bride belongs to the bridegroom." [4] Tears fell from my eyes as I realized that God was speaking directly to me. He was answering my question. The Almighty of the universe had revealed to me that Catherine was not just any bride; she was the Bride of Christ. Falling to my knees, I worshipped.

Several months later, I enlisted a local artist to paint a portrait of Catherine dressed in a wedding gown entering the Gates of Heaven. On the arch of the gate she inscribed, "The bride belongs to the bridegroom." I hung the picture on a prominent wall in our den as a reminder of God's unfailing love.

A Holy Boldness

Facing Cathy's death had the propensity to challenge the very fiber of my faith. I visited with some who had faced a similar loss and in the process, had struggled with their faith. Others, that I had spoken with, shared that their faith had grown cold—they were unable to reconcile why a loving God would allow such tragedy. For myself, my faith in God grew deeper and more passionate, and as God continued to reveal Himself to me, a new relationship was forged. I found myself loving Him with a depth I was unable to comprehend. I began to know Him intimately and personally. I liken His character to that of a respectful gentleman, never forcing Himself on me, but always desirous of my company.

Then, as God began to form a story in me, a noticeable change occurred. My questions changed. No longer did I seek answers to why God had allowed the accident. Now I asked, "How can I respond to this tragedy in ways that will glorify God?" I felt God stirring in me and the more I sought Him, the more I heard His voice. The more I praised Him, the more He gave me a new song to sing. In place of bitterness, He produced sweetness and I entered into what I now refer to as a "Holy Boldness." After reading Jesus' admonishment to His disciples not to worry about what they would say or how they would say it,[5] I felt confident He could do the same for me. At each opportunity that God provided, I posed the same question. "Are you ready to meet your Maker?" At the darkest time in my life, God opened doors for me to proclaim His Glory, and as I obeyed, the void in my life slowly filled with a new purpose for living.

The first opportunity came much too soon, and the circumstances were anything but desirable, but I could not stand back. As I mentioned earlier, Joe, the state trooper, who met Mark at the scene of the accident the next morning, would grieve the loss of his sixteen-year-old daughter, Katie Jo, just two months later. She was involved in a single vehicle accident while on her way to school and suffered a fatal head injury. The death of a second teen in such a short time wreaked havoc with the already vulnerable youth in our community. As they attempted to reconcile such loss, they were confronted with the gospel message both of these young women had openly confessed. In their devastation, they witnessed the hope exhibited by both of our families. As the youth began to question what "truly mattered in life," the things of this world lost their hold on their lives and a personal relationship with Jesus Christ took on new meaning to many of them. As two families, we had the honor of encouraging these youth in their walk with the Lord.

The following month, a neighboring church asked me to speak at their women's Thanksgiving gathering. In preparation, I asked the Lord to allow me to speak with *great boldness*.[6] That evening I shared the painful details of Cathy's sudden death, and as the women listened, I believe they understood the urgent need to be ready to meet Jesus at any time.

Later in the spring, I travelled to Chicago with my husband, who was attending a business conference. It was like a mini-retreat with God for me. Away from the demands of daily life, I sensed God placing a vision for women upon my heart. The outcome was an all-day-women's retreat that focused on the importance of women's ministry within the church. Most of the women of our local church were able to participate.

I continued to seize the opportunities God presented. The adolescent girls of our church expressed a desire for an event that would speak to the issues they were facing in their daily lives. From that request, the women in our church banded together and planned a retreat we called "Princess for a Day." The girls were pampered throughout the day, enjoying manicures, massages, and hairdos, interspersed with sessions of praise and worship and significant messages. The evening culminated with a bridal fashion show and with me as the keynote speaker. My message focused on what it meant to be the Bride of Christ. Using a portrait of Cathy as a backdrop, I was able to convey the message, that although youth and beauty are highly valued attributes in our society, neither had saved Cathy from death. I closed the evening by sharing the

Gospel message and giving them an opportunity to accept Jesus Christ as their Personal Savior and thus become the Bride of Christ.

Death lost its sting as God gave me victory through Jesus Christ.

Celebrating Birthdays

At one time, birthdays had been occasions for celebrating life, now they were times for sorrowing, yet always rejoicing. Birthdays signified life, but daily I was grappling with death. Those first birthdays hit hard and fast, beginning with Cathy's own birthday, barely two days after her death. Being a large family, the constant stream of birthdays was a challenge. With each birthday, I found myself comparing the years of "that life" against the years of Cathy's life. Death had created a new set point—now things were calculated by "before and after" the accident.

It was my constant desire that my remaining loved ones would know how much I valued them, yet Cathy's death threatened to consume me.

The Lonely Journey

"Loneliness is a cry of the spirit.
It does not demand answers. It just is.
Piercing, penetrating, unbidden."[7]—A. Irene Strommen

Journal entry: September 10, 2000

I walk so alone.
Nobody knows my pain.
Working with the past every day.
Sorting pictures, sending thank-you notes.
Sorting her bills, sending out death certificates.
Trying, struggling to keep up with every day.
When all I want is to be alone,
Care for myself,
Grieve by myself,
Find some meaning in this pain.
O Lord, giver of my soul,
Please rescue me from the depth.

That First Christmas Eve Without Cathy

That first Christmas Eve fell on a Sunday and I wrote the following letter throughout that day:

Dear Church Family:

It is Sunday, Christmas Eve. My first Christmas without my daughter. I woke early this morning. The tears were already on my cheeks. The loss will be my companion throughout the day, just as it has been for many days now.

I am waiting for you. I embrace my crying husband, console my youngest daughter, but I am waiting for you.

I know you have gone to the House of the Lord today. I couldn't; my strength must be measured out carefully today. I must conserve, so that I can meet the many needs of my hurting family.

I am watching the clock. I notice that you are still praising the Lord, but I am holding on. I need you to come … I need you to leave your fear behind and trust God that He will give you the words, if there are any. I need to feel your strong arms around me. I am hurting.

I have made my traditional Norwegian bread; my husband helped. Today, all of the chores will need many hands to complete. It is rising, and I am hopefully waiting.

I have checked the clock … It is 11:15 a.m. I know church is over … Surely you will not forget me today. Perhaps you had errands to run. Surely you are coming.

I have showered, I have dressed, and I am waiting. I don't understand why I need you, but today I need the human arms that God has created. I need you to bring me your Jesus. I need you to share His love with me. Today I need more than your prayers.

I understand that you are scared. I am, too. I wonder how I will hold up through the festivities of these days. The Merry has been taken out of Christmas. What I hope for is blessedness. Jesus said, "That whatever you do unto the least of these, you have done for me." Today, I am the least of these. I am waiting.

You did not come.

During the good times in life, I had enjoyed an abundance of friends, but now in death, only a few precious ones had the courage to stay nearby. Perhaps fear drove them away. Perhaps I drove them away. Perhaps they were looking for the old me and didn't realize the new me needed them more.

Death created a distinct loneliness and although my entire family experienced the loss, each of us had to wrestle through the grief individually. It was easy to feel abandoned, cynical and bitter, but by fixing my eyes on Jesus, He spared me from the further loss those feelings would produce.

Laughter—An Unexpected Gift from God

After such a painful Christmas Eve day, who would have imagined that God would give the gift of laughter at the Christmas Eve service?

Very much in touch with our stark loss, it was a tough decision to attend the service, but tradition and the need for a break from our anguish beckoned us out.

In Nicholas Wolterstorff's book, *Lament for a Son*, he says, "When we gather now there's always someone missing, his absence as present as our presence, his silence as loud as our speech. Still five children, but one always gone. When we're all together, we're not all together." His five children—our once six—how we identified with his words. Nicholas went on to say, "It's the *neverness* that is so painful. *Never* again to be here with us—never to sit with us at the table, never to travel with us, never to laugh with us, never to cry with us, never to embrace us as he leaves for school, never to see his brothers and sisters marry. All the rest of our lives we must live without him. Only our death can stop the pain of his death. A month, a year, five years—with that I could live. But not this forever." [8] Our hearts were overwhelmed with grief and sorrow to the point of despair. The earlier days of numbness were beginning to wear off. The *neverness* was quickly becoming a reality.

Now, had you been a church mouse observing our family that night, you might have shaken your head and commented, "This is not good." One daughter sat solemnly in the pew with a roll of toilet paper on her lap, a few seats further down sat another holding a whole box of tissue. The evening appeared bleak. Mark's head hung so low his eyes were invisible to anyone passing by. The church body was conscious of our pain.

The service began with the opening prayer, followed by Scripture readings, Christmas carols, and then special music, the source of our laughter. I intend no disrespect. Perhaps the laughter was an indication of our emotional state on that particular Christmas Eve. The duet began; it was discordant and harsh to the ears. It continued. Was it possible for it to get worse? Evidently yes! The dissonance provoked a reaction in each of us. Laughter spilled out—hearty, uncontrollable laughter. The saving grace that night was the realization that it is nearly impossible to differentiate between laughter and weeping, so long as one kept their head held low. Our bodies shook as we attempted to muffle our amusement, and by the grace of God, we were not found out. Who would have imagined laughter would be our Christmas gift from the Lord.

As we left the service that evening, we were refreshed in an unimaginable way. Praise be to the God of Comfort, who knew our need to laugh again.

Cath, my dear, I wonder, were you laughing with us in heaven?

Christmas Journal Entries

We lit your candle at your place tonight, the candle you gave me last Christmas. The flame danced uncontrollably. It flickered and fluttered—I wonder were you there? Was it a sign?

It is hard not understanding the realm in which you live. If it were not you controlling the flame, then perhaps it was God Himself reminding us that you do live on.

Christmas morning, your dad and I were awake first. No loud music today. No merriment! We showered and dressed before we even left our room. Things were not the same. All the gifts under the tree were remembrances of you. Pictures, photo albums, clothing, books, ornaments— all pointed to you. No one even complained when I took pictures. We all knew they could be our last.

The next day, I said to Keri, "We got through it; perhaps it was even a little better than imagined." She replied, "But it didn't feel at all like Christmas."

That is so true. I did all the right things; I decorated, shopped, wrapped, baked, cooked, played more Christmas music than ever before, but it was so hollow, so empty. It was a day to remember Jesus' birth only.

As I write, I am thinking, "Come, Lord Jesus, come. I am weary of this journey."

Designing a Headstone

With the dawning of the New Year came the task of choosing a headstone. The unnaturalness of the duty made me feel crabby and irritable, after all, parents are not supposed to bury their children. Mark and I hiked through snow-filled cemeteries together, trying to get a feel for our taste in headstones. The dilemma was—this was not just any headstone. This would be our daughter's headstone.

Our children were all home for the holidays, creating an opportune time for us to decide on the particulars together. Knowing the sales rep eased our discomfort slightly, but still, as we sat around our kitchen table, there was tension in the air. There were so many options to consider. Did we want a family headstone? Did we want an individual headstone? Did we want a headstone at all, or would we rather have a simple grave marker? Did we want granite, bronze or marble? After much discussion, we settled on a medium sized black polished granite headstone with an open Bible and a cross intertwined with ivy between the pages, an image of her face, her name and birth date, the date of her death with the epitaph "Gift of Grace" all etched into the surface.

In the end, we felt the headstone would honor Cathy and her faith. The headstone was set in place for Memorial Day.

A Mother's Yearning

Cathy's death had come so suddenly and there were so many things I longed to tell her. I found it helpful to journal as a way to express some of the depth of my heart. I wrote the following letter to Cathy several months after her death:

Spring 2001

Dear Cathy,

Where does one begin—what is there to say that has not already been said? People say that when someone dies, things are left incomplete—words unsaid.

We had so many dreams for you, so many wishes that will never come true. How I wanted to see your face as you received your Board of Nursing results. You were such a wonderful nurse. It is hard for me to think that in only two more months, you would have been graduating as a registered nurse.

Cathy, I wanted to see you walk down the aisle in a flowing white wedding gown. I know your dad wanted the privilege to give you away, to trust Jered to take care of you. I wanted, in time, to watch you grow with child and experience your excitement as your baby gave its first kick. I wanted to see your eyes shine as you looked into your little one's eyes, for I knew at that moment, you would have realized in a new way, how very, very much I love you.

I wanted to see you blossom in all areas of womanhood. I knew you would have many hard choices to make. You were so gifted, much would have been asked of you, and you would have been left to decide between what was better and what was best.

I am glad for the days we had together, the love we shared, the special moments, the happy events, the little secrets, the dreams and the plans. I am so thankful for every little memory. My life is forever changed. My priorities, my values, my thoughts, my cares—they are so different now.

I wanted to be a part of your future. Now you have gone away and never again, on this side of heaven, will I feel your embrace, smell your sweet smell, touch your beautiful hair, hear your melodic voice, or listen to you tickle the ivories of the piano. So much loss—yet I hold fast to the hope of our reunion together in heaven, the thought of spending eternity together.

I want to thank you for the joy I had in raising you. You were such a delight, such a gift, and I always knew that. It was as though you were sent from heaven just for enjoyment. As I had said so many times in the last year of your life, if I were ever to rename you, it would have to be "Grace" for you have surely been grace to me.

My dearest Cathy, although we have said unwanted goodbyes much, much too soon in life, I will always treasure you in my heart. You have opened the gates of heaven, and I long for the day when I can once again hold you in my arms. I love and miss you so much.

Mom

My First Dream

At the time of Cathy's death, I imagined she would be constantly in my dreams. I remember being fearful that I would relive the accident in my sleep. Surprisingly, that was not the case. Cathy did not enter my dreams until eight and a half months after the accident.

It was Palm Sunday and I had been awake and had fallen back asleep. In my dream, I was looking in a mirror as I was getting ready for church. Suddenly, I saw another person's reflection. This person had a perfect body and I peered closer to grasp what I was seeing. Then I realized I was looking at Cathy. She looked the same as I had remembered her, except that her body and complexion were flawless. I reached out to hug her and drew her close to myself and we began hugging one another. I began to apologize for not hugging her more often. She replied by saying, "Mom, you did hug me often." She appeared contented and happy. Then she told me, "Mom, not everyone is here." I seemed to understand that she meant, not everyone I had expected to be, was in heaven. She then began reciting Psalm ninety-one and I was aware there was an association with her funeral. Then I woke up.

Throughout the dream, I knew she had left us. I knew it was only a dream, but still, it gave me a euphoric feeling and the sense that I had actually been in her presence. The memory of her hug lingered and I cherished it. At church, later that morning, Pastor Scott commented on my radiance. The dream had been so real, I felt as though I was still glowing and it gave me a renewed sense of peace.

I have had other dreams since then, but none have been comparable to that first one. I marvel at how God knew I needed a hug that Easter season.

The First Easter

Good Friday and Easter took on a new, profound meaning to me as I realized that all of my hope stemmed from those events. I pondered what it meant for Jesus to lay down His life as atonement for our sin and what a great gift He had bestowed upon us. I saw Easter through new eyes and gained a fresh appreciation.

The worship committee had erected a simple tomb at the front of the sanctuary with the stone rolled away and our family placed a large floral arrangement full of brightly colored spring flowers in the opening, in remembrance of Cathy and in celebration of her new life.

Easter bunnies, eggs hunts and baskets all took a back seat in the season.

The Grave Site

The cemetery, in which Cathy is buried, is nestled away deep in the woods away from the distractions of life. We had beautified her grave by planting a perennial garden on top of it and placing a park bench alongside it. I imagined myself spending many reflective moments there. However, I found myself fearing coming face to face with a bear and lost my courage to be there alone.

Later that fall, friends who lived close to the cemetery, asked me if I spent much time there. I responded by telling them about my fear of encountering bears. They looked at me with surprise written all over their faces and proceeded to tell me about the mama bear and her cubs that had been in that general area all summer. Immediately, I realized how God had protected me.

Many people find a sense of tranquility by visiting their loved one's grave, but for me, my greatest peace is realized when I am reaching out to people in need and attempting to make a difference in their lives. Cathy was a loving, compassionate child who gave freely of herself to others. I feel that I honor her life when I, in turn, follow her example. In that sense, I understand the words of Isaiah 11:6 where it says, "a child will lead them."

The First Anniversary

As the first anniversary approached, a spirit of heaviness settled upon my heart and an unexplained dread filled me. As a family, we planned special ways of honoring Cathy's memory. We created a full-page memorial complete with pictures and remembrances for our local newspaper. I painted small wooden hearts a bright yellow, embellished them with daisies and ivy, and left them at the grave for visitors to sign and leave behind as a memorial.

Jenn and her two daughters flew home to be with us and each of us took the anniversary off of work. On that morning, we gathered at our home and solemnly walked together carrying flowers and balloons to the site of her accident. A painted wooden cross marked the place and served as a reminder to those passing by. We attached balloons to the cross and released the remainder in the air, watching them climb higher and higher, secretly wondering if they would reach the heavens. My mind flashed back to a year earlier, as I remembered Cathy being lowered deeper and deeper and the balloons soaring higher and higher.

Then we went to the cemetery with more flowers and balloons. We took family pictures around her grave, but the headstone bearing her picture was a poor substitute for her presence. We left the basket of wooden hearts for others who might stop by on this day.

We returned home and shared stories and memories and tried to remember her final words to each one of us. Each of us thought back to what we had been doing at the time we heard the news. It was morbid, yet somehow fitting.

The evening was rainy and dismal, as though mimicking our feelings. As the hour of her death drew near, we once again walked contemplatively down the highway to the scene of her accident. Each person carried a battery-operated candle and we walked in a single file line. Those passing us in their vehicles, slowed down, as if to remind us they had not forgotten our loss. Gathering around the wooden cross, we sang "Amazing Grace" as we had a year earlier at the graveside. Slowly and tearfully, we trudged home again—broken in spirit, but thankful for each other.

Acquainted with Death

After a year of being impacted by death, speaking about it felt relatively normal and oftentimes we would forget that others who were not journeying with us had difficulty even broaching the subject.

We wanted to do something special to honor Cathy's would-be twenty-first birthday, so we decided to go out for dinner together and invited Jered and his family to join us. Christy, being the family baker, once again made a special cake to honor Cathy's memory.

We arrived at the restaurant, our arms laden down with babies, diaper bags and the cake. When our waitress saw us entering, she quickly rushed to the door and offered to put the cake in the kitchen until later.

We enjoyed reminiscing together over our meal. After the waitress cleared the table, she returned with the cake and candles. Holding out the cake she innocently asked, "Who is the birthday girl?" Our three young granddaughters chimed in unison, "Cathy!" Then the waitress mistakenly asked, "Which one is Cathy?" The girls replied in staccato, "She's not here. She's dead. She's in heaven." That poor waitress, it is a wonder that she didn't drop the cake right there. I highly doubt she will ever willingly carry out a birthday cake again.

For our grandchildren, death had become a fact, a reality, a natural part of their daily conversation and they had no reservation in speaking about it.

Summary

The first year, came to an end and by the grace of God, we had survived all the *firsts*. Individually, we could testify to the faithfulness of God in our lives and with that, I could only imagine things becoming easier, that somehow the worst was behind us. I was sorely mistaken. The first year had been cushioned by numbness and denial, but now those too were about to be stripped away and the *neverness* would become more real.

Although the tragedy had radically altered the direction of our lives, it would take more time to fully appreciate the power of Jesus in His present risenness.

The threads, though accumulating, did not yet resemble a tapestry.

A Pilgrimage Through Suffering

Pilgrimage: religious journey—a journey
to a holy place,
undertaken for religious reasons.[9]

Walking through grief has been a pilgrimage, a holy journey, religious in the sacred sense. I have learned much on the journey and the loss has drawn me into a closer relationship with the Lord. In the book of Corinthians, the Lord says to Paul, "My grace is sufficient for you, for my power is made perfect in weakness."[10]

I consider it a great privilege to share some of the things I have pondered as I have journeyed with my Lord.

A Paradox—Peace and Pain

"The promised peace
that the world cannot give us
is located in being in right relationship
with God."[11]—Brennan Manning

Journal entry: 09-15-2000 During the hard lessons of life, I realize God is in control. He can take care of my pain and give me meaning in the loss. I don't understand why I haven't felt anger or the need to ask "Why me?" questions. At the scene of the accident, I experienced perfect peace— which of course is the peace that passes understanding. In spite of knowing God is in control—the earthly loss, the pain, the being robbed of her future, causes me excruciating pain—a paradox of peace and pain.

Journal entry: 12-06-2000 We watched the movie Shadowlands *last night, the story of C.S. Lewis' journey through death. In reference to death, he made the comment to a group of placating scholars, "It's bloody awful!" Those words captured my sentiments.*

"If you believe, you will receive whatever you ask in prayer."[12] Lord, today I ask for peace—peace for myself and for Joe and Joan; the peace that passes all understanding.

What is peace? Is it the calm that quiets the storm in my heart? The still, small voice that says, "It is well with my Soul?" Is it the hope that shines in the distance, even though a storm rages within me? "My peace I give to you, my peace I leave you." [13]

Journal entry: 12-07-2000 *The pain in Mark's eyes is almost more than I can bear. I feel helpless. I want to do something for him. The song, "The Altar," by Ray Boltz is playing softly in the background. The words, "Take your burden to the altar" are resonating in my mind. "O Lord, lift up Mark today."*

To experience such excruciating pain and yet remain at peace is a paradox that defies earthly reasoning. Perhaps it is most simply a provision of God's grace. The other day I looked through the photos that were taken by law enforcement at the scene of the accident and I was confronted by how "bloody awful" the scene actually was. Viewing them is painful, but it does not diminish my sense of peace. I really have no way to explain this except that it passes my understanding.

Witnessing My Children's Grief

"Crisis always reveals a person's true character."
—Oswald Chambers

Journal entry: 11-13-2000 *I am overwhelmed with grief as I pray for my children. My eyes well up with tears, as I think of their pain and know I am unable to bring healing to them. I want to fix them. Yet God tells me, "They that wait upon the Lord will renew their strength."[14] The depth of this loss is unfathomable. If it were not for the Lord, it would consume me.*

Living with my own pain was somewhat manageable, but witnessing it in my children was sheer agony that often brought me to my knees. As a mother, I was accustomed to attending to my children's wounds, but this wound rendered me helpless.

In Romans, God uses suffering to produce "perseverance; perseverance, character; and character, hope."[15] To watch suffering move through the many stages is heart wrenching, but to see the finished product is astounding. The changes I have witnessed in my children are remarkable. They have attained a maturity beyond their years. They have become more sensitive, more compassionate, more thoughtful, and more heavenly minded.

I praise God for His tender mercies and His unfailing love and I thank Him for fixing what was beyond my ability.

Regrets

Journal entry: 11-13-2000 I was talking to Christy on the phone yesterday and she told me how her roommates had shared with her that Cathy wished I had called her more. She went on to say that Cathy didn't get as many letters as the other girls, and how when the phone rang, Cathy would jump up to answer it saying, "Maybe it's my mom." Oh, the wretched agony of knowing I can never make that call again; the realization of what I have lost on this earth. "Lord, it hurts so much. Help me to remember to reach out to my remaining children."

Journal entry: 12-04-2000 As I begin my journal, I could easily label this chapter "Regrets." We spent the weekend in Grand Forks, the four of us, with Christy joining us whenever she could. How I regret that Jenn and Laurie could not be with us. We came specifically to attend our first Lorie Line Concert in memory of Cathy. My heart was heavy as I walked through the stores, finalizing Christmas gifts. Cathy loved Christmas. It feels as though I have lost my heart for Christmas.

I have found myself regretting.

I am walking through the mall regretting that I didn't call Cathy more often, wishing that I could tell her how much I love her, wishing that I could feel her embrace one more time and wishing that one more time I could hear her say "I love you too."

I regret that we never went wedding dress shopping— just for fun. Cathy loved weddings. We had spent so much time talking and planning her wedding. I remember the one weekend we spent every possible minute talking. Cathy had thought Rocky Point would be a great place for a wedding reception. She had been so excited to go back to college and talk it over with her friend, Ivy.

I regret the day Cathy invited me to go to Thief River Falls with her. I couldn't, because I had to work; three days later she died.

This morning I remembered her last hug and kiss goodbye. How I regret going out that night. If only I had stayed home, the course of history would have been changed.

Death stirs up so many feelings and at times, I find myself asking the question, "Is there really a God? Does heaven truly exist? Or I am just fooling myself into believing?" Praise God! He can accept my momentary doubts. In fact, He often counters them by reminding me of the times in my life where there was no question as to who God was.

Still there is the pain, the loss—the regrets.

I read an excellent book by Gerald Sittser called, *A Grace Disguised*. In it, he makes a weighty statement about the significance of our choice in facing regrets. He says, "The difference between despair and hope, bitterness and forgiveness, hatred and love, and stagnation and vitality lies in the decisions that we make about what to do in the face of regrets over an unchangeable and painful past. We cannot change the situation, but we can allow the situation to change us. We exacerbate our suffering needlessly when we allow one loss to lead to another. That causes gradual destruction of the soul."[16] This profound statement challenges how we proceed in light of regrets. Life offers us many choices, but our choices are not without consequence.

The Sacredness of Tears

"There is sacredness in tears.
They are not the mark of weakness, but of power.
They speak more eloquently than ten thousand tongues.
They are messengers of overwhelming grief, of deep contrition, and of unspeakable love."
—Washington Irving

Journal entry: 08-15-2000 *Another morning. I didn't cry yesterday. The busyness of the day took away my reflection time and I didn't have time to think about Cathy. It makes me feel guilty.*

Tears are a gift. Tears remind us we are truly alive and that we care. Albert Smith says, "Tears are the safety valve of the heart when too much pressure is laid on." I have often found having a good cry provides a sense of relief. Sometimes you may feel embarrassed if you cry around certain people and you may be inclined to repress your feelings. It is important to remember that our emotions are a gift from God. They set mankind apart from the rest of God's creation. God has designed us with the capacity to love and hate, laugh and cry, and sorrow and rejoice. Our tears are so precious to God that according to Scripture, He saves them in a bottle.[17]

When someone would endeavor to talk to me about my loss, and I could see that their desire to show love surpassed their fear, I would experience a sense of warmth and acceptance that allowed me to talk about my feelings.

Tears spoke a language of their own. When a friend would cry with me, I knew they had entered into my sorrow and for a few brief moments, the loneliness of grief was lifted.

Days without tears were often the most painful. Without my tears, I had a sense of detachment and emptiness. It was as though my tears validated my loss. The uncontrollable flow of tears remained only for a season.

God has promised that one day He will wipe away every tear from our eyes, and there will be no more death, no more mourning, no more crying, and no more pain.[18] What a glorious day that will be!

As I Embraced Grief

"Grief can only be embraced, never managed."[19]
—Larry Crabb

Journal entry: 09-01-2000 O Lord, this pain of mine, this loss, I need you to show me your purpose for my life, that Cathy's death might be of some lasting value. I want so badly to see her face again. I know you have a purpose for me here. "Show me your ways, O Lord, teach me your paths." [20]

"Do not conform any longer to the pattern of this world, but be transformed by the renewing of your mind. Then you will be able to test and approve what God's will is, His good, pleasing and perfect will." [21] *Is God telling me*

I need to look at Cathy's death through His eyes? Does He have a model for grieving that He wants me to follow?

The following is a short list of what grief accomplished in my life:

> Grief confirmed that I had deeply loved.
> Grief exposed my brokenness.
> Grief stripped away all pretense in life.
> Grief shattered my ideology.
> Grief challenged my outlook.
> Grief forced me to examine my purpose in life.
> Grief brought me to a place of helplessness.
> Grief incited me to cry out to God in deep anguish.
> Grief drew me to the cross.

Grief removed my desire to be conformed to this world, replacing it with a desire to be transformed by the renewing of my mind.[22] God used death to open my eyes to the brevity of life in comparison to the span of eternity. He helped me to see that each day is truly a gift from God and each of us has only one chance to use it. We are all of intrinsic value to God and His good and pleasing will is that all should come to know Him and that none should perish.

> Grief taught me how to seek God above all else.

Our Hope—The Secrets of the Vine

Christmas is a family time, and although Cathy is no longer with us in person, she remains with us in spirit. I can no longer give her material gifts, but I still desire to honor her memory. Cathy had a living hope in Jesus and the hope of eternal life based on her personal relationship with Him. Sharing Cathy's story with others often opened the way for me to share the hope that God had given us. While pondering the impact of

Cathy's life, I wrote the following Christmas letter to my husband and children and gave it to them along with a copy of Bruce Wilkinson's book, *Secrets of the Vine*.

Christmas 2002

Dear Family,

I have wondered over these last months how to celebrate the memory of Catherine at Christmas. I know each of us is still very much grieving the loss of her. I have contemplated how much we loved her and thought about all that we have in common as members of her family.

When I think of Cathy, I often think of ivy and vines, as clearly she loved to decorate with them. The thought struck me that the very thing that we all have in common is "the Vine." Our hope comes from knowing we will see Cathy again in heaven. The Vine is what makes that possible.

Jesus says, "I am the true vine, and my Father is the gardener. Remain in me, and I will remain in you. No one can bear fruit by itself; it must remain in the vine. Neither can you bear fruit unless you remain in me. I am the vine; you are the branches. If a man remains in me and I in him, he will bear much fruit; apart from me you can do nothing" (John 15:1, 4–5 NIV).

It is my hope and prayer for each one of us that we will learn the "Secret of the Vine" in our personal lives, so that when we are called home to be with the Lord, we will have much fruit. The only true hope for healing in our lives is to reach out to Jesus and allow Him to touch our hearts. Never will we ever forget Cathy. She was a part of us, and on this earth, we will always feel the gap that she left in our lives. However, I am so thankful for each of you. Each time I look into your eyes or hear your voices, my heart is uplifted. I have learned the truth about what matters; things are nice to possess and worldly aspirations are there to chase after. The dreams we have on this earth are all gifts from God. We have a right to pursue them and enjoy earthly happiness, but in the end, our relationship with the Vine is what will allow us to live together eternally.

Each of you is so very, very precious to me. I want to thank you this Christmas for all the joy that you have given me and will continue to give. One of us is missing, but we are still a family. We still have a purpose, and each of us is still an integral part of each other's lives. I am praying that God will bless each of you in this New Year as you have blessed me in this past year.

Love now and forever, MOM

Seven Years—July 27, 2007

It is seven years today. I thought it would be easier. I thought the raging battle was over, but here I am missing Cathy with a new intensity. I have planned too many activities this week. I am wishing I had planned some solitude.

Reminiscing has brought on insomnia and anxiety, reducing me to a state of helplessness, competence to incompetence, confidence to uncertainty. What are these emotions that rage in me? Where do they come from? What purpose do they have?

In my pain, I called out for protective prayer this week and a dear friend responded by sending me the following prayer.

Father, take her hand just now as she reads this. You know, O God , how the flies of the enemy swarm and threaten to suffocate us. Help us to remember that they are just flies and will die with a swat. We know that your hand is in this and Your purposes, far from being worried, are perfect and perfected in weakness. So we give you our weakness and do not own it ourselves. Our lives are hidden with Christ in You. Mystery to our mind—but joy to our hearts. Praises and blessing to you, my King.

Once again I find myself at the foot of the cross calling out to my Abba Daddy, "Please hold me closer. Please shoo away the flies and receive my weaknesses as an offering. Surround me with your presence. You fought the devil with 'It is written.' May I also cling to what is written?"

The Voice That Speaks in the Dark

What I tell you in the dark, speak in the daylight,
what is whispered in your ear proclaim from the
roofs (Matthew 10:27 NIV).

Earlier in this book, I stated that every preconceived idea I had about God would be challenged on this journey, bringing me to the place where I would embrace God as He is, not as I had perceived Him to be. I have reached that place and in doing so, have humbly asked God to reveal the falsehoods I have clung to and replace them with His truth. The time had come to let God speak and I was prepared to listen. It was time to face the hard questions. Now, more than ever, I was ready to hear the Master's response.

The following entries are a direct response to my attempt to embrace God as He says He is. With fear and trepidation of misconstruing His Word and its intention, I humbly share my observations with you.

"Theology becomes rich only when it survives the onslaught of pain. And sound theology leads us through our pain to a full experience of Christ, and therefore of hope and love and joy." [23]

The Sovereignty of God

"What God in His Sovereignty may yet do on a world-scale I do not claim to know; but what He will do for the plain man or woman who seeks His face I believe I do know and can tell others. Let any man turn to God in earnest, let him begin to seek to develop his powers of spiritual receptivity by trust and obedience and humility, and the results will exceed anything he may have hoped in his leaner and weaker days. Any man, who by repentance and a sincere return to God will break himself out of the mold in which he has been held, and will go to the Bible itself for his spiritual standards, will be delighted with what he finds there." [24]—A.W. Tozer

As I turn in earnest to God, seeking godliness with a desire to develop spiritual receptivity by trust, obedience and humility, the results exceed my expectations. What I deem true about the Sovereignty of God directly influences my perception of life, but it does not alter the Sovereignty of God. With those thoughts in mind, I purpose to move beyond what *I believe* to seek Him who is Truth Himself.

> The Lord brings death and makes alive;
> He brings down to the grave and raises up.
> The Lord sends poverty and wealth;
> He humbles and He exalts.
> He raises the poor from the dust
> And lifts the needy from the ash heap;

He seats them with princes
And has them inherit a throne of honor.
For the foundations of the earth are the Lord's;
Upon them He has set the world (1 Samuel 2:6-8 NIV).

I believe that the Lord is absolute. It is His prerogative to choose for His creation a time to be born and a time to die. Cathy's death challenged my beliefs. All my life I had firmly believed that you could not die a day before your time. This was the first belief to be tested. Were these words merely lip service? Did I truly believe that Cathy's life was in God's hands, not the driver's or fate's? Did I truly believe nothing happens without God's permission? Did I truly believe that God was in control and all things work together for good to those who love Him? Did I truly believe that God could bring good from death?

And still there were more questions I had to wrestle with such as, "What kind of God is it who could intervene and save an innocent child from death and chooses not to? Who is this God who pours out this precious perfume, who wastes this treasure of immeasurable value? How can I understand? Will I ever understand? Do I need to understand?"

O God, I must seek foremost to know You. I lay down my questions and confess my guilt before you. Who am I to raise a fist to You? I want to see You. Please take my eyes off my loss and fix them on You, the Author and Finisher of life. Forgive my insolence. Help me to seek you diligently, no longer the image I have created, but You alone. I have heard you telling me, "You will seek and find Me, when you seek Me with all your Heart." [25] *O Lord, this death has brought me to this place where I do seek You with all my heart. O Lord, it is time for You to strip away what I have clung to and expose the error of my way. You have said no one can lay any foundation other than the one that is already laid, which is Christ Jesus.* [26] *Lord, demolish this building I have created with my own hands and erect a new dwelling place on a solid foundation, fit for You to dwell in. God, I ask You to take captive my every thought. Reveal to me the high places in my life that I have failed to remove, the things that hinder my spiritual growth. Expose the sin that is unaddressed in my life.*

Dr. Normal Geisler in his *Systematic Theology* says, "God's Sovereignty is based in several of His attributes, especially omnipotence, omnibenevolence, omniscience, and His omnisapience. Since God is all-powerful, all-good, all-knowing, and all-wise, He both knows the best thing to do and has the power to do it. Further, since God is before all things, created all things, upholds all things, is above all things and owns all things, He is the rightful ruler of all things." [27] Dr. Geisler uses big words, because He is defining a big God, based on the Word of God. I know God is Sovereign and He is willing to give me wisdom and understanding, if I will look to Him, if I will set aside my preconceived ideas and be open to His teaching.

I want the foundation for what I believe about salvation, eternal life, and heaven to be consistent with God's Word. The Bible teaches that God is Sovereign and in His Sovereignty, He knows all things. God's Word teaches that He has a purpose that includes knowing the beginning from the end. In my finiteness, I have tried to understand this, but I have fallen short and in doing so, failed to see God's bigger plan. I thought this world was everything; I thought it existed for my enjoyment. Unintentionally, I have been guilty of laying up treasure where moth and rust can destroy. A tiny window is opening and I can see another whole dimension. This is my time to lay up treasure that will not perish. I have lived as if this existence was the promised banquet; now I see this is but a foretaste of what is to come. God in His Sovereignty has been preparing me for more. My questions have stemmed from my ignorance, but God has been waiting patiently for me to turn and seek Him with all my heart.

God says He sees even the little sparrow that falls. How much more was He aware of Cathy's whereabouts that night? I now realize God in His Sovereignty had declared Cathy's earthly work complete. God is not a glorified Santa Claus, who has come to make all the little boys and girls happy. He is the Creator of the universe, whose purpose is to conform me to the image of His will, that I might bring glory to His name.

I have read my Bible in its entirety many times. I believe that God is who He says He is, and that He is in control. These beliefs are as foundational to my Christian walk as breathing is to my physical existence. Without them, I will surely find myself doubting the goodness of God. When I fail to fix my eyes on God, my circumstances become my compass and then I find myself struggling to see His purposes for my life. When I turn toward God, He allows me to see things in a new light. Once again, I find the words of Gerald Sittser very fitting in my life. Speaking of the accident that robbed him of three generations of his family; his mother, his wife and his daughter, he says, "Much good has come from it, but all the good in the world will never make the accident itself good." [28] I, too, concur, that much good has come from Cathy's accident, but the accident itself was not good. God used Cathy's death to help me take my eyes off temporal things and in turn, place them on things of eternal value. I rest in the knowledge that God, in His Sovereignty, knows what is best for me and what will be most productive in helping me find His purpose for my life.

I Tell You the Truth

Jesus answered, "I am the way and the truth and the life. No one comes to the Father except through me." (John 14:6 NIV)

What *has* God promised me? What can I expect from Him? Do I know God well enough to answer to these questions?

In the four Gospels, Jesus says, "I tell you the truth" seventy-eight times. What is the truth He is referring to? What difference does it make? The thesaurus uses these words as synonyms for truth: fact, reality, certainty, accuracy, genuineness, precision, exactness, legitimacy, veracity, honesty, candor, integrity, dedication, loyalty, devotion, fidelity, uprightness, sincerity. What I believe is *truth* defines how I view life and death. Understanding what God has established as *truth* is foundational to a Godly perspective.

What constitutes truth, versus what I think is truth? What authority establishes truth? If one argues that there are no absolutes, does that claim make the argument valid? No. I need to look at the claimants and the basis of their authority. Jesus claimed that all authority in heaven and earth was given to Him.[29] It is not my intent to give a defense for what I believe; many fine scholars have written such a defense. If you find yourself questioning the truths of Scripture, I encourage you to read *The Case for Christ,* by Lee Strobel, or *Evidence That Demands a Verdict,* by Josh McDowell. My stand is based on the authority of Scripture.

I found great comfort in the many areas that God spoke to me through His Word, I found that *"the truth"* set me free.[30] When I read that Jesus found the disciples asleep, exhausted from sorrow,[31] I realized that there was a correlation between my exhaustion and my sorrow. I found consolation and freedom in the Scripture, "…godly men buried Stephen and mourned deeply for him."[32] If godly men mourned deeply, then it was not wrong for me to mourn. The testimonies of Biblical characters who had suffered were a solace to my soul. The Psalms of David gave credence to my grief and fellow sojourners that I could identify with. Jesus' words to the thief on the cross, that today he would be with Him in paradise,[33] gave me assurance that *today, not at a future date, but right now,* Cathy was in paradise with Jesus. The *truth* renewed my hope and gave me purpose and direction in my life.

A Story to Tell to the Nations

Journal entry: 08-14-2000 *The song "We've a Story to Tell to the Nations" is resounding in my mind.*

After the accident, a particular tune kept playing over in my mind, but it wasn't until a few weeks later that I was able to put a name to it. It was an older hymn called, "We've a Story to Tell to the Nations." As I reflected on the lyrics, I wondered if God had a purpose in bringing it to my mind.

Death had changed my outlook on life and I found myself seeking meaningful involvement with people. As a result, I began helping with the teen ministry at our church, and ultimately had the privilege of leading a youth team to Mexico for a short-term mission's trip. It was a special blessing to have two of my daughters participate, Christy, as a chaperone, and Sarah, as a youth. The trip had a great impact on the team, but even more so on Christy. After returning home, she felt a call to minister to the Mexican people. As we began to explore the options, she discovered that the mission we had gone out under had an immediate need for a teacher capable of teaching English as a second language. Since Christy had recently graduated with a degree in education, she was a good fit for this ministry. She had fifty-one days to raise her support and arrive at the training center.

A church we had previously pastored heard of Christy's intentions and invited her to come and share about the mission. Desiring to be a help to her, I accompanied her to the service. While sitting in the familiar sanctuary, my eyes wandered forward to the pew where we used to sit as a family. It was close to the pulpit, a place that had given Mark a clear view of his young daughters, all six of them. My heart ached for those days and my eyes filled with tears. Christy finished her presentation and returned to the seat beside me. The congregation rose and began to sing, "We've a Story to Tell to the Nations." My mind flashed back to three years earlier and suddenly I understood His purpose in placing that song in my mind. Jesus had been preparing me and showing me that we had a story to tell to another nation. First, He had sent Christy, Sarah and myself; now He was sending Christy. She would go to another nation and tell the story of God's faithfulness. Sorrowing, yet rejoicing, I could see God's plan to bring beauty from the ashes.

Heaven

"Heaven is our Father's house, the eternal destination of all believers in Jesus Christ. There are no mortgage payments in heaven. Our home was bought and paid in full by Jesus Christ." —D. Mark Watson

Can I believe that heaven is real, not some fable for the disillusioned? Can I believe it is more than merely mankind's attempt to lessen the sting of death? Can I be sure of heaven, where no eye has seen, no ear has heard, nor no mind has conceived what God has prepared for those who love Him?[34] Can a place so ethereal exist?

My hope is rooted in the Word of God and there, God promises that He has prepared a place for me in heaven.[35] Paul assures me in his Letter to the Thessalonians that we will be with the Lord forever.[36] John, in the book of Revelation,[37] tells me that God will wipe every tear from my eyes and there will be *no more death or mourning or crying or pain*, for the old order of things will have passed away. He goes on to describe this new heaven with streets of pure gold, and a city that does not need the sun or moon to shine on it, for the glory of God gives it light, and the Lamb is its lamp. Later, he says, "Nothing impure will ever enter it, nor will anyone who does what is shameful or deceitful, but only those whose names are written in the Lamb's book of life."

Without a doubt, I can and do believe that such a place exists and based on the Word of God, I am confident that Cathy is spending eternity with Jesus. Moreover, because I have a personal relationship with Jesus Christ, I look forward to one day joining her in heaven—my future home.

Comfort

"Our hearts of stone become hearts of flesh when we learn where others weep."[38]—Brennan Manning

Praise be to the God and Father of our Lord Jesus Christ, the Father of compassion and the God of all comfort, who comforts us in all our troubles, so that we can comfort those in any trouble with the comfort

we ourselves have received from God. For just as the sufferings of Christ flow over into our lives, so also through Christ our comfort overflows. If we are distressed, it is for your comfort and salvation; if we are comforted, it is for your comfort, which produces in you patient endurance of the same sufferings we suffer. And our hope for you is firm, because we know that just as you share in our sufferings, so also you share in our comfort (2 Corinthians 1:3-7 NIV).

I envision God's comfort with the memory of my granddaughter, Ryan, and her mother, Jenn. One day following Cathy's death, Jenn had been sitting in the chair in the living room, crying. Ryan, only two and a half years old at the time, looked at her mom with concern, and asked, "What's wrong, Mommy?" Then she placed her chubby hand on Jenn's cheek and lightly stroking it said, "It will be ok Mommy."

I am amazed at how wonderful it is to be comforted by those who have received comfort from God—the One Who is Comfort, and the One Who Comforts. Bill and Enid, Mike and Mary, Bryan and Mary, Norm and Ruth, Kathy and Jake, Jack and Rose, Dave and Myrna, Shirley, and others I am unable to recount— you brought comfort to us from the comfort you had received; and your testimonies renewed our hope. I can only imagine the camaraderie our children share in heaven. Thank you.

And to those who have become fellow sojourners, I thank God for the opportunity to share His comfort with each of you: Pastor Scott and Linda, Steve and Donna, Joe and Joan, Mark, Janet, Mary, Denise, to name a few. Your children have joined the great cloud of witnesses in heaven. I pray that God will use you to comfort others with the comfort He has given you.

It seems appropriate to add this postscript at this time. This past week (2009) we stood with dear friends after a tragic accident took the life of their eighteen-year-old son. The night of the accident, Clint's grandpa said, "God is speaking." Five days later, over four hundred mourners, more than half of them young adults gathered to remember his life. And God spoke again—He gave an invitation to each person to enter into a personal relationship with Him.

I tell you, now is the time of God's favor, now is the day of salvation (2 Corinthians 6:2b NIV).

The Role of Angels

This discussion deviates somewhat from the former topics in this chapter, but since it was an area of great controversy among the youth following the deaths, I would consider it negligent if I did not address it at this time.

After Cathy's death, there were many conversations about the role of angels. This topic often lacks serious study and consequently it leads to confusing beliefs and heresies. For this reason, I chose to include a few personal thoughts. Consider these two events:

On February 14, 1999, we received a long-distance call telling us our daughter Christy had been involved in a car accident. She lost control on an icy road and rolled her vehicle a minimum of three times, landing upside down in the ditch without the protection of a seatbelt. Upon impact, the windows caved in and Christy crawled out through the rear window of a still running car with minor injuries. Were there angels there to protect her? Did they help her out of the vehicle? I believe they did.

On July 27, 2000, Catherine was rollerblading and struck by an oncoming vehicle, causing instantaneous death. Were the angels there? Yes, I believe they were, but it was Catherine's appointed time to die. Did the angels have a ministry at the scene of the accident? Yes, I believe they carried Cathy home to heaven and then positioned her earthly body in the ditch in such a way to protect us from seeing the full extent of her injuries. The angels were also there to comfort and minister to us in our loss.

Angels do have a purpose, but we do not define it. Norman Geisler in his *Systematic Theology* series says that God created angels to glorify God, to serve God, to reflect God's attributes, to learn God's wisdom and grace, and to minister to God's elect. There are many scriptural references to angels throughout the Bible. A word of caution—be careful not to concoct a doctrine to support your opinion; instead allow the Word of God to teach you. Always ask the question, "What does God's Word teach?" My desire to embrace God as He is, not as I had perceived Him to be, has helped me to discern the truth.

When considering the role of angels, it is easy to fall prey to deceptive philosophies. When Cathy died, I wondered if perhaps she had become an angel. At the time, it was a comforting thought; I even mentioned it at the funeral. Further study exposed errors in my thinking. I discovered that angels do not share in regeneration and that one day believers will judge them. Billy Graham, in his book, *Angels, God's Secret Agents,* says, "Although angels are glorious beings, the Scriptures make it clear that they differ from regenerated men in significant ways. How can the angels who have never sinned fully understand what it means to be delivered from sin? How can they understand how precious Jesus is to those for whom His death on Calvary brings light, life and immortality? Is it not stranger still that angels themselves will be judged by believers who were once sinners? Such judgment, however, apparently applied only to those fallen angels who followed Lucifer." [39]

Dr. David Jeremiah, in his book, *What the Bible Says about Angels,* points out, "Everything Scripture says concerning angels is in connection to something else as the main theme. There are no pages or passages whose central purpose is to spell out a doctrine of angels." [40] Later in the discussion Dr. Jeremiah says, "Anyone who delves into a study of angels with a high view of God will come away with an even higher view."[41] He goes on to admonish, "Much that goes on in the name of angels in our world isn't biblical; we need caution not to get caught in the web of angelmania. Whatever our past experiences or beliefs or opinions regarding angels, they must be checked against the principles of Scripture. They must spring from Scripture, not from what we have conjured up in our minds that we'd *like* to believe about angels." [42] We need to exercise godly discernment when we are looking at such things. The Word of God is to be our final authority.

Fred Dickason, in *Angels Elect and Evil,* does an excellent job of paralleling the ministry of angels to the ministry of the Holy Spirit. "Scripture indicates that the ministry of angels to men is primarily external and physical, whereas the ministry of the Holy Spirit is internal and spiritual. Angels minister *for us*; the Holy Spirit ministers *in us*. They guard our bodies and pathway; He guards our spirits and guides us in the right way. They may be agents to answer prayer, but He is the Prompter and Director of our prayers." [43] We would do best to keep our attention focused on *"the Prompter and Director of our prayers."*

This chapter opened with a quote by Larry Crabb and I find myself coming back to the same as I end this chapter. These are penetrating words that I understand so much better now than before. Thanks Larry.

"Theology becomes rich only when it survives the onslaught of pain. And sound theology leads us through our pain to a full experience of Christ, and therefore of hope and love and joy."

Reflections of New Desires

Now we see but a poor reflection as in a mirror;
then we shall see face to face.
Now I know in part; then I shall know fully, even
as I am fully known (1 Corinthians 13:12 NIV).

This journey has inspired many new desires within me. It has also helped me to release some of my dearly held beliefs, and unleash my desire to speak the Word of Truth boldly.

This chapter is dedicated to sharing the new desires that God has inspired in me. Desires to dream better dreams, to pray better prayers, to love God more, to reflect His image through my life, to be joyful in hope, to be patient in affliction, and to be faithful in prayer.

To Dream Better Dreams

"You are never too old to set another goal or
to dream a new dream."—C.S. Lewis

The clock of life has continued to tick, never missing a beat. The hours roll into days, the days into weeks, and the weeks into months. With time, the pain has lost its razor-sharp edge. It has become more like a shard of glass weathered by the friction of sand and water. Once the edges became smooth, they no longer could cut to the quick.

Although I still miss Cathy, it is different now. I used to fear forgetting, *forgetting her voice, her face, her smile ...* I now know I will never forget these things and in that, I am set free to remember the beauty of her life and embrace the wonderful memories.

This journey has taught me lessons that now influence my daily choices. Now, I am more inclined to dream better dreams, as I daily choose to live my life to the fullest, to glorify God in and through the things that I do, and to live with eternity as a focal point. I want to champion my adult children and their spouses to grasp for better dreams. I want to encourage my parents to live their life to the fullest. I want to stimulate a desire in my co-workers to seek Christ as the answer to their problems. I want to motivate the Body of Christ to move toward one another in a way that kindles community. I want to learn to dance with the Trinity. These new desires inspire my dreams.

My days are numbered, and I want to make them count. "You do not have, because you do not ask God. When you ask, you do not receive, because you ask with the wrong motives, that you may spend what you get on your pleasures."[44] I want to have the confidence that I am asking God for the best things with the right motive—things that will endure.

After Cathy's death, I cried out to the Lord, "Make my life count, make it meaningful, or get me out of here." Recently, I asked God to forgive me for my selfishness and show me the purpose He has for me. When I die, I want to hear, "Well done, my good and faithful servant."[45]

To Pray Better Prayers

"What seem our worst prayers may really be, in God's eyes, our best. Those, I mean, which are least supported by devotional feeling. For these may come from a deeper level than feeling. God sometimes seems to speak to us most intimately when He catches us, as it were, off our guard."—C.S. Lewis

Who would imagine that death would inspire me to pray better prayers? Suddenly, the prayers for safety, for comfort, for blessing are second things in my heart. I want to know what it means to pray in the Spirit in such a way that "streams of living waters flow,"[46] to pray for a godly response to trials, to pray for those I love, prayers that make a difference in their lives. I want to pray in a way that my Father in heaven receives honor and glory.

This morning, while ironing and praying through my prayer list, God inspired me in a new way. I had a vision of keeping a prayer journal for each grandchild, a journal where I could record my thoughts and prayers for them. I rushed out to the store and purchased nine journals. It is my desire to pray for them that they might turn to the Lord while they are still young.

While reflecting on my grandchildren, I thought of words such as birthright, legacy, and heritage. When you grow up in a Christian home, you should expect to have a general knowledge of the things of God. You should know there are no second generation Christians—that each person must come to the place in their own life that they make a personal decision to follow Jesus Christ. I am so thankful for my heritage and pray that I will leave a Godly legacy behind.

When I pray with the sincere desire to know God's will and to live according to His ways I can trust that God will be at work in my heart.

To Love God More

"Knowing God is life's major pursuit,
but that's only half the story.
Loving God is our ultimate response."
—Chuck Swindoll, *Living Insights*

Journal entry: 12-08-2000 *"Love the Lord your God with all your heart and with all your soul and with all your mind"* [47] *All your heart—all your soul—all your mind—three distinct aspects of our being that influence our capacity to love the Lord.*

Seven years have slipped by and once again, this verse in Mark is challenging me. "To love Him with all your heart, with all your understanding and with all your strength, and to love your neighbor as yourself is more important than all the burnt offerings and sacrifices." [48] I find myself asking God, "What are the burnt offerings and sacrifices I am offering You? What religious things and ways of thinking are hindrances to my relationship with You? Knowing You has become a major pursuit in my life, but how far short have I fallen in loving You? Lord, I ask that you might teach me *how* to love You."

To Reflect His Image

"One of life's greatest paradoxes is that it's in the crucible of pain and suffering that we become tender. Not *all* pain and suffering, certainly. If that were the case, the whole world would be tender, since no one escapes pain and suffering. To these elements must be added mourning, understanding, patience, love, and the willingness to remain vulnerable. Together they lead to wisdom and tenderness." [49]

God does not take us into the crucible of suffering without a purpose. His ways are not our ways. He is a purposeful God. There are lessons for us to learn. This season of pain and suffering has been fruitful in my life. I have learned to cling to the Father, and in doing so, He has blessed me in ways that I could only previously imagine.

In the crucible, much was stripped away. Death brought brokenness to my life, unlike any other circumstance. Pain poured out from me; I felt destroyed by adversity. My life turned upside down. Self was emptied, and the remaining, shattered pieces of my life were laid bare.

Jehu Burton in his book, *Trusting through Tears*, says, "Suffering is God's most effective tool for conforming us to the image of Jesus Christ. God puts His workers through the refining fire; the greater the mission, the hotter the fire. Nothing changes a person more quickly or more completely than suffering. Nothing alters one's perspective or values faster than suffering. Complete value systems can be changed in moments when one becomes immersed in suffering." [50]

Suffering opened my mind to a new way of thinking. God became the center of my life, not merely someone to fall back on. He opened my eyes to see how temporal this life is and to see the value of living for God. He took those remaining shattered pieces of my life and molded them into a new vessel, ready to serve Him.

> *Praise be to the God and Father of our Lord Jesus Christ! In his great mercy he has given us new birth into a living hope through the resurrection of Jesus Christ from the dead, and into an inheritance that can never perish, spoil or fade—kept in heaven for you, who through faith are shielded by God's power until the coming of the salvation that is ready to be revealed in the last time. In this you greatly rejoice, though now for a little while you may have had to suffer grief in all kinds of trials. These have come so that your faith—of greater worth than gold, which perishes even though refined by fire—may be proved genuine and may result in praise, glory and honor when Jesus Christ is revealed. Though you have not seen him, you love him; and even though you do not see him now, you believe in him and are filled with an inexpressible and glorious joy, for you are receiving the goal of your faith, the salvation of your souls (1 Peter 1:3-9 NIV).*

I received the following email from a friend.

> *Malachi 3:3 says, "He will sit as a refiner and purifier of silver." This verse puzzled some women in a Bible study and they wondered what this statement meant about the character and nature of God. One of the women offered to find out the process of refining silver and get back to the group at their next Bible Study. That week, the woman called a silversmith and made an appointment to watch him at work. She didn't mention anything about*

the reason for her interest beyond her curiosity about the process of refining silver. As she watched the silversmith, he held a piece of silver over the fire and let it heat up. He explained that in refining silver, one needed to hold the silver in the middle of the fire where the flames were hottest as to burn away all the impurities. The woman thought about God holding us in such a hot spot; then she thought again about the verse that says: "He sits as a refiner and purifier of silver." She asked the silversmith if it was true that he had to sit there in front of the fire the whole time the silver was being refined? The man answered that yes, he not only had to sit there holding the silver, but he had to keep his eyes on the silver the entire time it was in the fire. If the silver was left a moment too long in the flames, it would be destroyed. The woman was silent for a moment. Then she asked the silversmith, "How do you know when the silver is fully refined?" He smiled at her and answered, "Oh, that's easy—when I see my image in it."[51]

If today, you are feeling the heat of adversity, remember that God has His eye on you and will keep you under His watch until He sees His image reflected in you. How I pray that my heavenly Father might see His image reflected in me!

To Be Joyful

"… our ideas about happiness need a major overhaul, and that only the suffering brought about by shattered dreams can do the job."[52]—Larry Crabb

Journal entry: 08-31-2000 "These things I have spoken to you, that my joy may remain in you, and that your joy may be full."[53] O Lord, this joy that I have in my soul I know flows from You. The loss is so great, yet the knowledge of Your love and care for us and for Cathy surpasses the grief. Teach me, show me, mold me, use me, and make me into a vessel for Your service. Lord, I desire You to return quickly, but ask that in Your waiting, many souls will be brought to You.

After Cathy's death, I found myself dealing with tremendous sadness. Oftentimes, I would break down crying. This happened one time when I was talking to my brother. My pain hurt him deeply and wanting to encourage me, he said, "I think God wants you to be happy." I was very angry at his suggestion and thought it was ludicrous that he would even make such a ridiculous statement. Happiness was not a desire in my heart. I hung up the phone and searched my Bible to see what God said about happiness. I felt that if God wanted me to be happy He surely would not have allowed Cathy's death. I knew God was in control and that everything happened for a reason, but I did not feel God expected me to be happy. I was experiencing the joy of the Lord, but that was different from my perception of happiness. Paul, in Romans, exhorted me "to be joyful in hope, patient in affliction, and faithful in prayer." [54] This I could handle, but happiness was something that I would have to wait for God to restore.

To Be Patient in Affliction

"Brokenness is realizing He is all we have.
Hope is realizing He is all we need.
Joy is realizing He is all we want." [55]—Larry Crabb

Journal entry: 10-04-2000 *"But the plans of the Lord stand firm forever, the purposes of his heart through all generations." [56] So Lord, this death, it was in Your plan—part of Your purpose. I trust Your judgment, but today I hate Your plan. Bear with me in my sorrow—be gentle with me. I know you questioned Job about his whereabouts when You set the world in place. I know You* *see the beginning from the end and I trust You—it is just that the pain and the loss is so great.*

Suffering is inevitable, and as Christians, we should not expect to be exempt. The Psalmist records, "Remember your word to your servant, for you have given me hope. My comfort in my suffering is this: Your promise preserves my life."[57] Job, in the midst of suffering said, "The churning inside me never stops; days of suffering confront me."[58] Paul spoke of "great sorrow and unceasing anguish in my heart."[59] Peter warned us by saying, "Dear friends, do not be surprised at the painful trial you are suffering, as though something strange were happening to you."[60] We have many Biblical examples of suffering.

Although suffering can be the result of sin, that is not always the case. In the Gospel of John, Jesus' disciples asked who had sinned, the blind man or his parents. Jesus replied by saying, "Neither this man nor his parents sinned, but this happened so that the work of God might be displayed in his life."[61]

God can use the suffering in our life to fulfill His purpose in us. When you encounter suffering, heed the words of James, "Consider it pure joy, my brothers, whenever you face trials of many kinds, because you know that the testing of your faith develops perseverance. Perseverance must finish its work so that you may be mature and complete, not lacking anything."[62] God is doing a maturing work in you so that He might display His sufficiency in you and through you.

Now if we are children then we are heirs—heirs of God and coheirs with Christ, if indeed we share in his sufferings in order that we may also share in his glory (Romans 8:17 NIV).

For just as the sufferings of Christ flow over into our lives, so also through Christ our comfort overflows (2 Corinthians 1:5 NIV).

To Be Faithful in Prayer

Previously, I addressed my desire to pray better prayers and explained what that meant to me. Now, I would like to address, my desire to be faithful in prayer, focusing more on the frequency of prayer. Perhaps the easiest way to explain the shift is by the following example. There was a time in my life that prayer was limited to table grace and bedtime prayers. Now, in contrast, my life is immersed in prayer. In 1 Thessalonians 5:17, we are called to, "pray continually." After Cathy's death, my prayers were continual. I found myself at a crossroads—no longer having answers to my questions. Things that were once so important, no longer seemed to matter. Out of sheer desperation, I began to walk in constant prayer and as I did, God revealed Himself to me. His Word became alive and our relationship changed. Praying continually was no longer a chore; it was a privilege. Now, I pray continually, not out of obligation, but out of a desire to know my Father more and to participate in the fulfillment of His will on earth. He is my life coach and I need to be in constant contact with Him.

I desire to do your will, O my God; your law is within my heart (Psalms 40:8 NIV).

Words of Insight for Fellow Sojourners

Hear my prayer, O LORD, and give ear to my cry;
Do not be silent at my tears; For I am a stranger with Thee,
a sojourner like all my fathers (Psalm 39:12 NASV).

The insights from fellow sojourners often illuminated my path and helped me to process my grief. With humility, I share some of my own personal insights with the hope that they might be of some value to other sojourners.

A Word of Advice

Journal entry: 09-15-2000 *"Loss is a universal experience like physical pain; we know it is real, because sooner or later, all of us experience it. But loss is also a solitary experience. Again, like physical pain, we know it is real only because we experience it uniquely within ourselves."* [63]

In my grief, I yearned for the companionship of others who had experienced the ravages of death firsthand. Although I knew individuals who were not strangers to death, it often seemed that they were reluctant to talk about their experiences; perhaps because it brought back painful memories. Still desiring the insights from others, I resorted to combing the shelves of Christian bookstores for books written from a Christian perspective by fellow sojourners.

Many of the books I read cited a staggering statistic, asserting that eighty percent of marriages, Christian and non-Christian alike, end in divorce following the death of a child. This reality caused me to take a closer look at my own marriage, as well as creating a desire to understand some of the underlying dynamics that might have contributed to this outcome. Because I never intend to be misleading, I do need to add, that later, when I was looking at some statistics online, the consensus was that this figure was grossly inflated and probably more realistically was twenty percent. Regardless, I do think the following observations have merit and are worth sharing.

After examining my own tendencies and observing other fellow sojourners, I noted several things that might be contributing factors. The death of a child is traumatic, and leaves you feeling vulnerable, lonely, and too exhausted to engage in personal relationships. Although both spouses may share the same loss, they may be experiencing different stages of grief, and hence appear insensitive toward each other. The spouse, feeling abandoned and neglected, may begin to withdraw emotionally from the relationship, setting the initial stage for divorce.

Returning to work, before we have had adequate time to process our grief, may be an instance when a spouse withdraws from a relationship. Males and females often use different coping strategies. Males more generally conceal their feelings. They are not used to sharing issues of the heart with each other. Therefore, in the workplace, the grieving male may feel alienated from other male co-workers who do not know what to say, so they say nothing at all. Or he might come up against those who turn the conversation to safe subjects, such as sports or politics, seeming completely insensitive to his loss. It may become easier for him to resort to avoidance tactics to mask his pain, longing for his workday to end, so he can escape to the safety of his home. If his home fails to provide a place of refuge, he may turn inward and thus be perceived as detached and uncaring by his spouse.

Women, on the other hand, more naturally reach out to one another on an emotional plane, and because of this, they are more likely to experience camaraderie among their female friends. The danger is in the fact that the more a female meets her needs outside of the marriage relationship, the easier it becomes for her to develop an unhealthy dependence on friends, and thus withdraw emotionally from her husband. A vicious circle, that unless broken, will leave both spouses in a lose/lose situation.

After a death, a spouse may wrestle with a sense of guilt over engaging in the physical aspect of the marriage relationship. They may feel that under the circumstances, they have nothing left to give, leaving the other spouse with feelings of rejection. With the bonds of intimacy being torn down one at a time, an already hurting spouse may seek relief away from the marriage. He or she may seek relief in another person, or through drugs and/or alcohol. Any of these options will have a negative impact on the already struggling marriage relationship.

Until we, individually, come to the realization that God, alone, can meet our deepest needs, we will continue to use coping mechanisms that fall short and we will continue to find ourselves dissatisfied by the outcomes. As we look to God and find our refuge in Him alone, we will find contentment and peace in our lives. This may sound like simplistic theology, but the fact remains that God offers the gift of Himself to each of us.

Pondering the very real threat to the marriage relationship, after the death of my child, brought me to my knees. There, I asked God to protect our marriage, give me wisdom, and make me sensitive to my husband's needs. In turn, I looked to God to satisfy my needs.

God has been faithful, and in spite of the storm, our marriage has grown stronger. God has drawn us into a deeper relationship with each other. However, the greater good is that God has drawn both of us into a deeper, more satisfying relationship with Him.

Please understand that my intention is not to present an authoritative study on this subject, but to hopefully point out a few areas that I sincerely believe could be major precursors to failure in marriage. My prayer for you is that you will allow God to use whatever loss you are facing to draw you into a deeper relationship with Him.

Strange Things People Say

Loving people say the strangest things! A friend said to me, "You don't know what God has spared Cathy from." Did he think that offered consolation? Another graciously reassured me that God needed her more, but I found no comfort in such a needy God. Others blamed Satan for her death, while others suggested I needed to get on with my life.

Realizing, that in my pain, I was more inclined to snap back negatively, I deliberately chose to be silent instead. The old adage *"bite your tongue"* was very good advice for me. Many times, that is exactly what it took for me to remain courteous. I truly believe that most people have good intentions, but their awkwardness with death leads them to say inappropriate things.

Regrettably, there have been times when I have found myself at a loss for words and voiced some of the same rhetoric. Realizing my insensitivity, I have found it necessary to apologize and ask for forgiveness. Love covers a multitude of sins and a genuine caring attitude is generally accepted.

I can assure you, well intending people will continue to say strange things, but you can use that to your advantage if you learn from it. My humble advice is to give careful thought to your own choice of words and remember a warm hug speaks volumes.

The Changing Faces of Grief

Journal entry: 09-12-2000

I love you O Lord my strength.
The Lord is my rock, my fortress and my deliverer;
My God is my rock, in whom I take refuge.
He is my shield and the horn of my salvation,
My stronghold.
I call to the Lord, who is worthy of praise,
and I am saved from my enemies.
The cords of death entangle me;
the torrents of destruction overwhelm me.
The cords of the grave coiled around me;
the snares of death confronted me.
In my distress I called to the Lord;
I cried to my God for help.
From his temple, he heard my voice;
my cry came before him, into his ears
(Psalm 18:1-6 NIV).

The memories of her death entangle me—not the picture of the actual accident, but the realization that she is gone. The grave reminds me of what I do not want to face. The loss and the pain are too much to bear on my own, so I trust God to rescue me. Even He seems far; I trust that He is working.

"At first grief wears a kind face, for grief begins with shock and numbness." [64] Then grief radically affects one's outlook. Life takes on a form of lifelessness. The heart feels clouded over. It is as though a new season has arrived, a bleak, harsh season. The sun does not shine, and the sky is continuously overcast. Heaviness hangs in the air. Exhaled sighs and sleepless nights accompany inner churnings. What you thought to be good has become suspect. The world appears different, as if you were viewing it through altered lenses. Grief threatens to rob you of future joy and desire.

Then one day a small bright spot appears. Perhaps it comes in a child's laughter or in a rainbow (a reminder of God's promises), or in a butterfly, bearing witness to new life. Slowly, you see signs that the season is changing. You want to welcome it, but you fear letting go. Grief has become your companion; you are familiar with its ways. To let go might mean forgetting, so you pull back. Then once again, you feel that nudge, and you step out to test the waters.

Slowly you realize it is *time*. With hesitation, you venture out with small baby steps. Cautiously, you embrace the new season; it is unlike any other season. It is filled with freshness, and so are you. You have become a deeper person. Grief has reshaped you. You now face life with a changed perspective.

I read in a book, "Time does not heal. The Holy Spirit heals. You choose to heal. Time only covers the event. Time puts distance between us and the event." [65] There is a profound truth in these words.

Understanding the Trauma of Grief

"Reason gropes in the dark for answers, faith waits for God." [66]—Joseph Bayly

We are accustomed to shouldering life's blows and quickly moving forward. Culturally, we are not encouraged to take time to sift through the interpersonal dynamics and emotional implications of our losses. A mere three-day leave of absence from work is not adequate time to process the event. We might find ourselves healthier and less stressed, if we had allowed ourselves a year of mourning. Although this may be idealistic and impossible, we must make the time to work through the loss.

Grief is not passive. It demands attention. Unheeded, it will find negative expression in our lives, perhaps manifesting itself as bitterness, anger, or anxiety.

Trauma and grief are closely intertwined. H. Norman Wright says, "Trauma shatters your beliefs and assumptions about life, challenges your belief that you have the ability to handle life, and tears apart your belief that the world is safe. Trauma leads to silence; you won't have the words to describe it. Trauma leads to isolation; no one seems to understand the experience you had. Trauma leads to feelings of hopelessness; you feel there is no way to stop what happened or the memories." [67]

Death can be especially traumatic. Time alone does not produce healing; nevertheless, recovery from unexpected, untimely death does necessitate time. It has been said that grief can take two to three years to work through; in the event of traumatic sudden death, that period is increased. Given that, we should not be surprised when grief appears to linger. If you find yourself depressed and losing perspective about life, you should seek counseling through your pastor, a trained professional, or your doctor. Talking about your loss can be therapeutic.

In my opinion, if you take the time to tarry in grief and seek God's counsel, He will restore you. Challenging your beliefs against the Word of God will strengthen you. As a shepherd uses his staff to draw his wandering sheep back to himself, so the Lord desires to use His truth to lead you beside still waters to calm and restore your soul. [68]

Then Comes the Morning

Weeping may remain for a night,
But rejoicing comes in the morning (Psalm 30:5 NIV).

I have come through the night, and the darkness has given way to the light of the morning. The tragedy radically altered the direction of my life, and I concur with Brennan Manning, that in my vulnerability and defenselessness, I have experienced the power of Jesus in His present risenness. I truly serve a risen Savior.

What Matters

"But the things that matter most in the world, they can never be held in our hand." [69]

Journal entry: 09-21-2000 *"There comes a place on our spiritual journey where renewed religious activity is of no use whatsoever. It is the place where God holds out His hand and asks us to give up our lovers and come and live with Him in a much more personal way."* [70]

Cathy's death has set me on a new journey; religious activity and things of this world feel so empty. At times, I am so happy for Cathy, and then at other times, as right now, I just long to see her face, to hear her voice, and to feel her warm body in an embrace. Cathy's death has shown me how temporal the things of this world are. Now, I can better see the things of lasting value. Like Paul, I believe the scales have fallen from my eyes, and I see life as I have never truly seen it before. We are indeed aliens in a foreign land, just passing through.

When death invaded my home, claiming the life of my child, I innately knew what mattered. All Cathy's accomplishments suddenly became past tense and the only thing that mattered was her eternal condition. It was only with an eternal perspective that anything made sense. With the assurance of Cathy's faith in God, I could have hope. Knowing, without a doubt, where Cathy stood with the Lord and having the assurance she was eternally with the Lord were the things that mattered. I am so thankful to know that Cathy had given her heart and life to Jesus, inviting Him to be her Lord and Savior.

Larry Crabb, in his book *Shattered Dreams,* shares these words spoken by a friend after the sudden death of her husband: "Everything's different now. What used to matter so much just doesn't matter in the same way. Nothing really matters now, but knowing God." [71] I agree—nothing really matters except knowing God, knowing that my loved ones know God, and knowing that Cathy knows Him and lives eternally with Him. "What good will it be for a man if he gains the whole world, yet forfeits his soul?" [72]

Come to Me All You Who Are Weary

"Our impulse to tell the salvation story arises from listening to the heartbeat of the risen Jesus within us. Telling the story does not require that we become ordained ministers or flamboyant street corner preachers nor does it demand that we try to convert people by concussion with one sledgehammer blow of the Bible after another. It simply means we share with others what our lives used to be like, what happened when we met Jesus, and what our lives our like now." [73]—Brennan Manning

Journal entry: 11-29-2000 Matthew 14:13 NIV "When Jesus heard what had happened, He withdrew by boat privately to a solitary place." Jesus had just heard that John the Baptist had been beheaded and as a result, he withdrew to be in a solitary place. I can identify, since Cathy's death, I have often desired to be alone. After reading the parallel account in the book of Mark, I more clearly saw Jesus' invitation to his disciples to "Come with me by yourselves to a quiet place and get some rest."

In the same way that Jesus invited His disciples to a solitary place, He extends the invitation to each of us. He beckons us throughout His Word with verses such as these. "Come to me by yourselves to a quiet place and get some rest." [74] "Come to me all you who are weary and burdened, and I will give you rest. Take my yoke upon you and learn from me, for I am gentle and humble in heart, and you will find rest for your souls. For my yoke is easy and my burden is light." [75] "The Lord your God is with you, he is mighty to save. He will take great delight in you, he will quiet you with his love and he will rejoice over you with singing." [76]

God has strengthened and renewed me, and now, I believe He is sending me to encourage my brothers and sisters with the comfort that I have received. It is my prayer that this testimony of His faithfulness draws you to the one and only God, that you have heard Him calling your name and inviting you to a solitary place. God shows no favoritism; all are invited. [77]

If you have never received Jesus Christ as your personal Savior, know that He is calling you today. He does not desire that any should perish, but that all should come to Him. [78] Today, wherever you are, at home, at work, or at play, Jesus is calling you to come to Him. You need only to invite Him into your heart— telling Him you recognize your need for a Savior. Although you have lived life in your own strength, you acknowledge that as sin, and you now hear Him calling you to come home. If today you hear His voice, I encourage you to pray this prayer:

> *Lord Jesus, I hear Your voice, I have lived life without You and I need You. I have chosen the empty things of this world to satisfy. Forgive me today as I see how sin has separated me from You. I invite You today to come into my life and dwell in my heart. Lord Jesus, I wait upon You for my strength. Amen.*

If you have invited Jesus Christ into your heart today, please know I would love to hear from you. Contact information is included on the final page of this book.

Journeying Back

As I have journeyed back, piecing together those dark days of grief, God has allowed me to see a more accurate picture of the devastation that took place in our home. I had assumed I had been there to shelter my children, as they received the horrific blow. It was painful to discover, that in reality, because I was a prisoner of my own pain, I was not emotionally there for them.

Writing this manuscript allowed me to revisit that night and the days that followed with each of my children and grandchildren. The necessity for accuracy created a safe place, where we were free to talk about some of the events that took place and how we perceived them then, opposed to how we perceived them now.

At times, in the medical profession, a doctor has to reopen and gently probe an infected area with a sterile instrument before re-bandaging a wound. This allows further healing to take place and reduces the risk of infection. Although it is never a pleasant procedure, at times it is necessary. God used the writing of this book in much the same way, and as a result our family has experienced healing at an even deeper level than before.

Each of us has survived. The fire and the flames that threatened to destroy us were the same threads that God used to refine us. God, in His infinite wisdom, continues to produce beauty from the ashes.

Where once only threads were visible, now a beautiful tapestry has taken shape.

The Unseen Tapestry

"We must watch closely as the tapestry is woven… or as it unravels." [79]—Randy Alcorn

A phenomenal thing has happened, as we have passed through many seasons, stages, and phases—even years, since that never-to-be-forgotten Thursday evening.

In the background, invisible to the human eye, God has been at work. Bound so tightly by the cords of death, we were oblivious to the faint threads He was weaving. Then, in an unforeseen moment, He drew back the curtain, and revealed His handiwork to us. Even now, as I share that unveiling with you, my heart is overwhelmed in gratitude, for I never expected, on this side of heaven, to understand with such clarity, what God was doing.

I thank you dear reader, for the time you have devoted to reading this story. Several years ago, we held a private viewing. Today, we throw open the doors and invite you to join us in worshipping the God of all comfort as you read these final pages.

The Unveiling

Therefore, since we have such a hope, we are very bold. We are not like Moses, who would put a veil over his face to keep the Israelites from gazing at it while the radiance was fading away. But their minds were made dull, for to this day the same veil remains when the old covenant is read. It has not been removed, because only in Christ is it taken away. Even to this day when Moses is read, a veil covers their hearts. But whenever anyone turns to the Lord, the veil is taken away. Now the Lord is the Spirit, and where the Spirit of the Lord is, there is freedom (2 Corinthians 3:12-17 NIV).

It was Tuesday, September 26, 2000—one day shy of the two-month marker of Cathy's death. I had returned home late the night before from a ten-day visit to Texas, my second visit in the past two months. Having had the opportunity to spend some personal time with Jenn and her family had left me feeling more at ease with her situation.

Although it was barely eight o'clock in the morning, my house had already emptied. Mark had taken the girls with him, dropping them off at school on his way to work. Pouring the first cup of coffee of the day for myself, I proceeded to make my way into the living room—ready to enjoy some reflection time with the Lord. As I was moving in that direction, a faint sound in the distance caught my attention and triggered an alarm within me. I felt a prickly sensation wash over me and the hair on the back of neck stood up. Now straining to hear, I set my coffee down and walked over to the picture window. Peering down the highway, my eyes latched on the accident site. I wondered if it would always be this way.

Suddenly I am flashing back. *I hear the sound of sirens getting closer and closer. My heart begins pounding in my chest. My eyes turn away from the accident site as I turn to look down the highway toward town. Now, I can see the flashing lights and hear the high pitch sound of the sirens. I watch as an ambulance speeds by, followed closely behind by a police car. Sickened by the memory, I try to shake it off—wondering if there will be an end to this torment. How long will this nightmare consume me?*

Then, it is as though I wake up—I realize this is not a delusion. This is actually happening! My imagination is not at fault. History is repeating itself; only the time of day has changed.

Out of sheer desperation, I begin praying aloud, "Lord, Lord, what is it that I am witnessing? How can it be happening again? O Lord, have mercy." The next thought that passes through my mind sickens me, dropping me to my knees. My arms unconsciously wrap around my body and I begin to shake as I am confronted by the question. "Where is my family—are they safe?"

The unvarying ticking of the grandfather clock at my side has now replaced the echo of the sirens. I remain on my knees; swaying back and forth in an even tempo until the ringing of the phone breaks through my catatonic state. I force myself to stand, unsure if my legs will hold me. I reach for the phone—caller id reveals it is Mark. My heart plummets and I feel lightheaded. Then I hear Mark say, "There's been an accident. It's a girl. It's Katie Jo Olafson." As he says her name, I can picture her the day she came over to share in our loss. She was wearing her denim overalls and her face was tender with compassion. I force myself to ask for details. Mark responds by telling me, she was unresponsive at the scene and they have taken her to Roseau Hospital where they will airlift her to Grand Forks. All I can think about is Joe and Joan. I remember our own devastation and I am sickened at the thought of theirs.

I try to pull myself together, so I can place a call to Christy. I know she will want to pray for Katie Jo and her family. I reach her as she is walking to her first class of the day. She quickly picks up the tremor in my voice and asks what is wrong? I tell her what I know about the accident. She asks me to keep her updated. Hanging up, she continues on to class, until she realizes she cannot stay there, she has to leave. The accident is too close—too soon. Memories flood her mind as she makes her way to hospital.

Arriving there, she goes directly to the intensive care unit where she queries a nurse about the family. They tell her a brother is waiting in a private room for Katie Jo and her parents to arrive. The nurse graciously guides her to the room and while they are walking, she tells Christy that a state patrol officer had picked him up at school, over two hours away and escorted him to the hospital. Christy opens the door to the small room and she sees that two bodies occupy the space. She readily discerns which one is Jared, Katie Jo's older brother. His large body is slumped over and he is holding his head between his hands. The officer who is waiting with him nods for Christy to enter. Jared hears the jarring of the door and looks up. Recognizing Christy, he stands. Instinctively, they move toward the other and wrap their arms around each other in a desperate embrace, but neither of them speaks. For the time being, their thoughts and feelings are kept under wraps.

The clamor of footsteps rushing by interrupts the moment and they turn toward the window, fixing their eyes on the activity outside the hospital entrance. Hospital staff helps lift the narrow gurney from the helicopter and quickly begins rolling it toward the intensive care unit. Jared and Christy have stepped into the hallway and they *distinguish Katie Jo's lifeless body as the gurney races past them. She appears small and frail—helpless. Questions loom. Fear crawls up their spines. What does this mean? Where will it end?*

Back in Warroad, I sit next to the phone waiting for an update. Marks calls home again to share a request he has received from concerned parents, who have opened their home to Katie Jo's classmates. They are ill equipped to deal with the trauma alone and have asked us if we are willing to help. I ask myself, "How can we help? What do we have to offer? How can we do this?" Our wound is still fresh—gaping—bleeding—raw, but we can do no less than what they have asked. I dress quickly and wait for Mark at the door. Together we go.

The kids begin to arrive, first two, then five, then carloads. They number over fifty. They are shocked. They look to us in search of answers. We have none to offer. We hold them in our arms, our tears mixing with their own.

The updates are not good: a head injury—a brain injury—unresponsive—comatose. Together we cry. We are there and they have received us. They are seeking hope. We represent hope. "How is this, Lord?… Cathy died, but we represent hope. God, you have taken their eyes away from death and fixed them on You. You are amazing."

The awaited call comes; Katie Jo is stable for now. Everyone disperses. Already it is night.

It is Thursday, the third day. *For a second time, the concerned parents open their home to Katie Jo's friends and again, they request our presence. The school is sensitive to the needs of the students and offers to bus them to this home.*

The prognosis has changed. Katie Jo's friends are scared and so are we. They gather around the beautiful grand piano in the open living room and "Threads of

Love"[80] fill the room. Our memories carry us back to a different time and it is Cathy we hear playing the piano. We are trapped between two places, the past and the present; both overflow with pain and suffering.

Now it is Friday, the fourth day. Katie Jo has held on. Do we dare to hope? Tonight is the high school homecoming and all the festivities that brings. The school administration wanted to postpone the event, but Katie Jo's parents have requested they proceed as scheduled.

Sarah has been diligently preparing for this night when she will fulfill Cathy's vision. Earlier this summer, she had spent countless hours at Cathy's side, watching as she choreographed the dance; never imagining that her attention to detail would allow her in turn, to teach the senior cheerleaders the dance in Cathy's place.

Unprecedented at our school, Mark opens the football game in prayer. God is speaking and He has a captive audience. At the close of his prayer, the cheerleaders release fifty balloons into the sky representing our prayers for Katie Jo. Then they step forward onto the field, dressed uniformly in the T-shirts we have provided. T-shirts bearing a picture of Cathy and the following inscription, "This was her time." Sarah, at the tender age of thirteen, leads them in the dance. It is a flawless performance.

It is Sunday, the sixth day. Until now, we have refrained from going to the hospital; fearing that our presence might be a reminder of death and cause them to lose hope.

We can wait no longer. Now is the time—Katie Jo is slipping. We sense that God has sent us. We enter into the intensive care unit; the area is indicative of trauma. Joe and Joan meet us and draw us into an embrace. We feel a tearing of our hearts. Our grief has become so entwined with theirs, it can no longer be separated. They lead us *back to share their Katie Jo with us. The softly lit room has a hush over it and everyone speaks only in whispers. The angel of death is awaiting his orders. Katie Jo appears to be resting peacefully in the bed.*

"Lord can You not awaken her? Why, Lord—You breathed life into Adam; you gave Lazarus back to his sisters. Lord, why don't you say the word, 'Talitha koum!' and let life spring forth?"

That is not Your plan. We see but threads, there is no beauty.

Monday morning—the angel of death has received his orders. *Katie Jo has passed into the heavenlies where Jesus was waiting to receive her. Cathy is there to welcome her. The heavens resound with joy, but earth reverberates with deep groanings.*

It is evening, Joe and Joan return home. *We are there to meet them. We don't want to be, but in spite of that fact, we cannot stay away. What have we to offer? How can we offer less? The northern lights dance in the autumn sky. Together, we stand beneath them marveling at the timing of such a display. It is a harsh grief, buffered by a quiet hope.*

It is Wednesday evening—the night preceding the funeral. *The family welcomes Christy's presence, as they search through Katie Jo's personal belongings with the hope of unearthing something precious. Flipping through the pages of a notebook, Christy stumbles upon a diamond. Again, the seemingly insignificant becomes sacred. Upon the pages of that notebook, Katie Jo, has inscribed a note of reassurance and comfort. In her own handwriting are these words, "When God calls, you go, no matter what the age!" God's presence is sensed in a real way.*

It is Thursday morning, October 5, 2000—Katie Jo's funeral and Sarah's fourteenth birthday. *An early* snow has fallen overnight leaving everything pristine white. The funeral has taken precedence over school and a thousand mourners file into the gymnasium. The loss of two teenagers in two months has created turmoil in the hearts of people in the community. Many are crying out to the Lord, saying it is too much for us to bear on our own.

It is as though God had chosen Katie Jo to display His magnificent handiwork. Only a child, barely sixteen, yet His testimony clearly etched on the pages of her life. Our family was honored to participate in the service: Christy and Sarah sang Cathy's song again, Keri composed a second poem to read, and Mark offered words of hope through the spoken word and song. Tragedy had brought our families together, grafting us into a strange oneness.

It is weeks later, our paths cross again. Katie Jo's classmates are in search of answers. They come to us pleading for help. They form a group naming it "Stay Together Bible Study" and it becomes a safe place for them to ask their questions and an opportunity for us to teach the truth. God assures us that Cathy, and Katie Jo's deaths, have not been in vain. God is reaping.

There is an interlude. Time passes...

It is three years later and God writes another chapter. It is "a boy meets girl story," but it is not their first encounter. This time nothing clouds their vision and they see one another in a new light. There is a short time of courtship. Love moves quickly beyond friendship to a desire for lasting commitment. There is a proposal, a ring, and a wedding. During the ceremony, two mothers approach the altar side-by-side and light remembrance candles together. Then, they return to their seats to witness their children's vows. A few months later, a picture of the bride and groom hangs on the wall with two sisters superimposed in the clouds, one above each of them.

Two more years have passed. *At this time, two mothers pace the hospital hallway together, waiting not so patiently. The sound of a sharp cry stops them in their tracks. They listen closely for a moment; their fear disappears as they hear the lusty cries of a newborn. They embrace, and marvel at the miraculous event. Their children invite them into the room as they present the wee one to his grandmothers. This 'wee gift' from the Lord brings further healing. Looking upward, you can almost see the two sisters, now aunties, peeking through the portals of heaven to witness the joyous occasion.*

There is another interlude. Time passes ... God is still reaping.

The wee child is now a young man. The forces of this earth are in a battle for his soul. The young man is questioning the Sovereignty of God. Sensing the conflict, his parents realize that "this is the time."*

The parents lightly tap on their son's bedroom door before cracking it slightly open. Hearing them, he picks up his head to look at them and they can see the turmoil reflected in his saddened eyes as he sits on the edge of his bed with his long legs dangling over the side. They long to restore him to the carefree child he was, not so long ago. They walk over to him, seating themselves on either side of him, they put their arms around his shoulder. He doesn't physically push them away, but they feel his rejection. Perhaps they should have spoken to him sooner; hopefully, they are not too late.

His dad takes the now-aged sheet of paper out of his pocket and carefully unfolds it before placing it into his son's hand. The son looks skeptically at it, but it isn't long before tears begin to pool in the corners of his eyes, as he rubs his thumb back over the date—August 1, 2000. He recognizes the year, but is puzzled by the actual date, that is until he begins to read the message. Then he remembers hearing of the impact that summer and fall had on his parents. Before this, he had never fully comprehended how entwined his aunties' deaths were and although the accidents took place before his time, he now feels connected to the loss.

As he continues to read, he realizes that his Auntie Katie Jo wrote this letter after returning home from his Auntie Cathy's funeral. God had unveiled to her that day things that require an eternal perspective to comprehend.

… The young man's heart is changed as God reveals the intricate tapestry to him. Humbled, and touched, he places his trust in the Lord Jesus. Now he knows in part, then he shall fully know.

The battle has been won. The heavens resound with joy, but earth's deep groanings have ceased.

We wait patiently for the final unveiling.

Then I heard every creature in heaven and on earth and under the earth and on the sea, and all that is in them singing, "To him who sits on the throne and to the Lamb be praise and honor and glory and power, for ever and ever!" (Revelation 5:13 NIV)

"The threads are being woven together. The tapestry takes shape. Yet what the Weaver's final product will be, we cannot yet know." [81]

As part of the healing process, God occasionally gave me a bird's-eye view of the work He was doing and by doing so, He increased my faith to trust Him with what I could not see. Then He gave me a vision of how much more He was capable of doing. Although, this final interlude is fictitious, I know that God is not limited and I can only imagine the plans He has for our future. Leif is still a wee lad, but we look to the future and pray that God, who so graciously touched our lives, will touch his life, and the lives of our family, those present now and those yet to come.

The tapestry is still being woven.

The Diamond

Written by Katie Jo Olafson

8-1-00

Wow, I look differently on life now! Today was Cathy Watson's funeral. Their family has such a strong faith, that's how they are getting through this. (By the way, in case I read this years down, or someone else reads this, Cathy was rollerblading and was hit by Scott Thompson's truck.) The Watson's know that Cathy is in a better place, and that keeps them going through this. It was so sad/scary, seeing her coffin. Yet, I knew that just her body was in there, & while her spirit was all around us. After her funeral, I was thinking, (I know, scary thought huh?). You never know when its your time to leave our temporary home and go to heaven, & I want everyone to remember me in a good way. I want people to remember me like they remember Cathy..... fun-loving, caring, considerate, compassionate, and dedicated to GOD. I want to live completly for GOD, and I want to tell people about GOD's love for everything. Today my dad told me that we must always trust in the LORD, (duh!), and always be prepared to go to heaven. I think a lot of people are prepared to go to heaven, but nobody is ever prepared enough for a loved one to go to heaven. its weird.... you say "I'm prepared to go to my home in heaven @ anytime," but when someone you know & love dies, you ask GOD, "why them? They were so young, it wasn't their time." Well, I hate to break it to some people, but not everyone lives to be 100! When GOD calls, you go, no matter what the age! Okay, Selena is coming over, gotta go!

"Katie Jo Olafson"

Closing Comments

Written by my loving husband, *Mark Watson*
father of our beloved daughters
and grandfather of our next generation.

I'm quite confident that the question looming in the minds of some readers is, "Where is her husband in all of this?" It's a fair question and I'll do my best in responding to it. When, a friend, after reading the manuscript, suggested to Deb that I write something and she asked me to, I was humbled. My heart is bursting with pride over this labor of love that Deb has poured herself into for the past year and a half.

My personal relationship with the Lord Jesus Christ has been stumbling along for the past thirty-three years and thankfully, I've learned a few things along the way about God, myself, people and the world in which I live. Coming to terms with the death of my daughter, Cathy, has been the most daunting experience of my life and continues to be a soul stirring, mind stretching and heart searching journey. Men, in general, go underground with their feelings and tend to work them through, while women, on the other hand, typically talk them through with whoever is willing to go the distance with them. There are exceptions in either case and I like to think that I might be one, as the father of six daughters and husband of one wife. By God's grace, I've moved along the continuum of life to a healthier place of personal expression.

Grappling with Cathy's death for the last eight and a half years has, at times, been gut wrenching. It has changed my life and it took me the first five and a half years to adjust to its impact. One of the most helpful things I did was to write my thoughts and feelings down in the form of letters to Cathy. My daughter Keri created a memorial page for her sister on a website called virtualmemorials.com on October 30, 2000. The first time I wrote in the Guestbook was on March 10, 2001. From that point on, until February 7, 2005, I wrote on this site frequently—what was on my mind and heart to Cathy. It provided a safe way for me to express my innermost thoughts and feelings and relieved me of the burden of having to contend with someone else's reactions to what I was saying. I could say whatever was there to Cathy without anyone around me feeling compelled to try and fix me or take my pain away or make me feel better. Being heard does not require a solution, it implores a caring presence. It's not a matter of having the right words to say; it's the importance of just being there and listening with a compassionate heart.

My beliefs, growing up, were shaped by what my parents taught me through their words and actions and what I learned in Sunday School, through the public school system, and from life experience in general. From the time I personally believed in Jesus Christ as my Savior and Lord, at the age of twenty four, my beliefs have been rooted in what God says in the Bible. What I've learned through sermons, Bible studies, in Bible College and Seminary, in my years of ministry as a Pastor, through my own personal Bible study and my life experiences as a child of God have contributed to the convictions I hold today.

There's a world of difference in these two belief systems. I believe God is the Creator and Sustainer of the universe and all that it contains and that He, therefore, is Sovereign over everything that exists and is the authority on what life is all about. God is my perfect heavenly Father who loves me with a relentless love, that nothing in all creation can separate me from (Romans 8:38, 39). I am secure in His love and significant in His plan for my life. This is the foundation God has laid for me and on which I have taken my stand.

I am comfortable with the fact that I don't have all the answers, because I know God does. I don't understand many things, but I know God understands all things. My knowledge is partial and my experience imperfect, but in Christ are hidden all the treasures of wisdom and knowledge (Colossians 2:3). Jesus is the only One who has ever lived a perfect life. My greatest need is God and my greatest hope is Jesus in Whom is found the true meaning and purpose of life.

I've learned how indispensible my relationship with God is, above all else. I've learned how valuable the lives of my wife and daughters are to God and to me, and how important it is for me to invest myself in them and in lives of other people, because that's what really matters in this life.

God is teaching me what unconditional love is and how to give it. This has been a struggle for me throughout my life. I'm learning what it means to accept people just as they are, to be the person God has made me to be, and to allow Him to be the Change Agent, not me. We are not defined by what we think, feel, believe, say, or do, but by God, who created us in His image (Genesis 1:27).

We need each other more than we are willing to admit and we have to offer our world what only we can give.

I am much more sensitive, now, in how I relate to those who have lost a loved one, because of my own loss, than I was before Cathy's death. It's amazing how important it becomes to be with those who know what it means to grieve the loss of a loved one. The need to identify with someone who knows your pain, because they have experienced it themselves, is so compelling.

Without hesitation or question, the most important lesson I have learned through Cathy's death is that God is all that He says He is and this is my greatest hope. Those who are willing to trust God's revelation of Himself in the Bible and place their faith in Jesus Christ will experience the reality of God's goodness, His grace, His love, and His peace.

It is my prayer, that this true story of God's faithfulness in the lives of our family, will touch the lives of those who read it and draw them into the presence of God and into an experience of His love for them in ways that bring encouragement, comfort and hope.

Our Family Now

Our once large household of eight has grown even more. God has added many branches to our family tree. We now number twenty-three, including Cathy, and the family continues to grow in both number and spiritual depth.

Mark (fifty-six years old), my husband of more than thirty-five years, continues to work at Marvin Windows and Doors. Although God has chosen this company to provide for us financially, Mark's heart is in ministering to God's people. Together, we have a passion to make God's presence known.

As for me, Deb (fifty-four years old), I work two days a week as a receptionist at Falk Dental. My heart's cry is to touch the world with the unrelenting, furious love of God.

Jenn (thirty-three years old), husband Joe, children Ryan (eleven years old), Reese (nine years old), and Max (five years old) all live twenty-five miles away. In 2002, Joe's employment afforded him the opportunity to relocate to Northern Minnesota, once again allowing us to be closer to one another. God is using Jenn to draw hearts to the Lord Jesus through her gift of music. As she seeks to know the One and Only, she matures into beautiful womanhood, reflecting the love and faithfulness of her Lord.

Laurie (thirty-one years old), husband Rhody, children Kaitlyn (fifteen years old), Savannah (thirteen years old), Tyler (five years old) Cameron (four years old) and Lauren (two years old) live a few miles from us. Laurie is a devoted mom with incredible responsibility and incredible strength. She is learning the role of the proverbial woman, that of putting her family before herself.

Christy (twenty-seven years old), husband Jared, and son Leif (two years old) live seven miles from us. Christy is expecting their second child. Jared and Christy both suffered the loss of a sister within two months of each other. Both were instrumental in consoling the other. In God's unique way, He has brought them together, and I believe He has a unique ministry for them. Their ability to love and comfort will bear much fruit.

Keri (twenty-four years old) and husband Travis, and daughter Liza (newborn) live seven hours away from us. Keri is our nurse, who chose to walk in her sister's footsteps. Through the loss of her sister, she has learned her own capacity to touch the lives of the ailing with the hope and love of the Lord Jesus. She is a gifted caregiver.

Sarah (twenty-two years old) and husband Justin have recently returned to Warroad. Sarah is expecting their first child. Facing death at the tender age of thirteen brought accelerated maturity into her life. Her heart is one that is ever reaching out to her husband, parents, sisters, nieces, and nephews. Her actions demonstrate her love of Jesus.

Coda

Photo Album

"Our Family Then"
Photo taken in 1998
It is the last photograph taken of us as a family.

"Cathy & Her Mom"

"Cathy & Her Dad"

"Cathy's Graduation Picture"
Photo taken by Ilene Olson, Nature's Photography

"Sketch of Cathy" by Sarah"

"Another Graduation Picture"
Photo taken by Ilene Olson, Nature's Photography

"Cathy & Her Dear Friend Charity"
Together they composed "Stay Together"
Photo taken by Ilene Olson, Nature's Photography

"Cathy & Jered 1998"

"Cathy & Jered Prom 2000"

"Last Picture Taken of Cathy"
Taken with Roommates Charity & Susie

"Jered with his wife, Joni, and two children Connor & Cami"

"Sisters at the Accident Site on the First Anniversary"

"Cathy's Grave & Headstone"

"Our Family Now"
Photo from Our Family Reunion 2008.
Photo includes my parents.

Glimpses of Cathy

It is a fact that you can take nothing out of this world,
but you can leave something behind.
This chapter is dedicated to
"what remains."

Catherine Denise Watson

July 29th, 1980—July 27th, 2000

A few days before Catherine's twentieth birthday, she said to me, "Mom, I am only going to be a teenager for a few more days." Little did we know that for us, she would remain a teenager in our hearts forever.

"Myself at Sixty-five and Beyond..."

In many ways Cathy's life was ordinary. She had dreams and aspirations for the future. She loved life and people.

In college, she wrote this short paper titled, "Myself at Sixty-Five and Beyond…"

I picture myself at age seventy-five. I have been married for fifty-two years and have three children, eight grandchildren, and two great-grandchildren. The most important people in my life are my husband and family, and my mother, who is ninety-eight years old and lives with my niece and her family. I see my children about three times a year. I usually only see my grandchildren when we get together for holidays, except for one granddaughter who lives in town with her husband and visits quite frequently. I am in fairly good health, other than some minor heart problems. Of course, my bones ache now and again, but I think that is just part of getting old. I am taking some pills for joint pain and an anti-arrhythmic for my heart. My husband has hypertension and is on several heart medications since his heart attack five years ago. Neither of us smoke, and we drink alcohol upon occasion, probably once or twice a week. We try to go for a half mile long walk every morning to keep in shape and keep the blood flowing, although it is enough of a workout just trying to keep up with our great-grandchildren! We enjoy playing bingo on Sunday nights at church, and we like to travel when we get the chance. We are both retired; my husband was a manager at Federal Express for about forty-five years, and I was a full-time registered nurse at the hospital here in town for about forty years and have worked part-time with volunteer activities in the nursing home for the last fourteen years. We still have money left in our retirement savings that we started when we first got married, and with that and our social security income, we do fairly well. We live in Bemidji, Minnesota, and have lived here since a few years after we were married. My hobbies are quilting, spending time with my family, and getting together with friends. I also like to garden and go fishing with my husband when we go to our lake cabin in the summer. I feel very satisfied with my life, and I feel that I was able to accomplish most of the things that I had hoped to do. I still drive, and we have one car, a boat and a motor home. My husband and I are still very close, and we enjoy having romantic evenings to ourselves now and again.

Cathy lived her life with a contented spirit and deep spiritual convictions. Her values were evident in her personal possessions, such as her handmade calendar embellished with Scripture verses, and her list of long-term goals that included two pairs of new jeans. Her friends said she had been their spiritual mentor, always ready to take a stand for what she believed. She possessed a maturity and understanding beyond her years.

"Where your treasure is, there your heart will be also." [82] Like Mary, I ponder and treasure these things in my heart.

Glimpses of Catherine from Her Diary

The following notation was penned in her journal at the end of her first day of college: "I miss my mom already, even though it has only been a day. I guess that is sort of pathetic, but oh well." A treasure held dear to my heart.

Cathy was famous for her lists, such as this list we found in her journal.

1. *Do you want to be able to wear the dress you like for your wedding, or just settle for one that fits? ([Beside the comment is a photo of a beautiful bride in her wedding gown.)*

2. *Do you think she eats eight meals a day? No! Three is normal. Don't always think about food. (Another beautiful bride is pasted opposite the comment.)*

3. *Look in the mirror. Are you happy? Were you happy with how you looked for Farrah's wedding? It wasn't that hard to do it!*

4. *You can have thin arms! Lift Dude's weights and do pushups.*

5. *You have had a flat stomach before! Remember how good it made you feel. Do 125 sit-ups.*

6. *For Farrah's wedding, you weren't embarrassed to wear a swimsuit and Christy's pants fit loosely. Do some leg lifts and intro Tae Bo.*

7. *Remember how much better you feel when you drink H_2O. Try to drink four good glasses a day.*

8. It is so beautiful outside. Take three walks this week.

9. Eat three normal meals with two normal snacks, and don't eat after work.

10. No more than two hours of TV a day—wasted time.

11. **Read at least one chapter in the Bible—only takes five minutes.** [Emphasis added.]

12. Read a little school work each day (spend twenty minutes.)

13. Do something you have been putting off for a long time.

14. Give plasma one time a week. It is helping you and someone else.

15. **Pray before you shower and floss before bed.** [Emphasis added.]

This list was indicative of the way that Cathy embraced life. She challenges us by how naturally she included God in her everyday life.

Stay Together

Written by Cathy Watson and Charity McLaughlin

When I was just a child, a lifetime seemed to be forever.
And I was not alone,
'cause friends could always pull together.
Growing up together, we laughed and played
and never thought the world could ever harm us.
We had hopes and dreams and nothing in our way.
And we can make it through if we hold on to each other
We must always stay together.

Live for today …
you never know who might not see tomorrow.
When things don't go your way,
you need love to help you through the sorrow.
Live what you believe … you never know
when someone else just might be following your lead
into this world of pain and suffering.
But we can make it through
if we hold on to each other…
We must always stay together.

Now we've come this far,
And we will go our separate ways to meet our future.
Though the road is long,
we can spread our wings and fly out on our own.
We can make it through if we hold onto each other…
We must always stay,
No matter what comes our way…
We must always stay together.

Scholarship Letter

This letter was written by Cathy on December 22, 1999 as part of her application for the Dr. Russell O. and Inez Sather Scholarship.

I am currently a student in my second year of the Practical Nursing program at Northwest Technical College in East Grand Forks, Minnesota, and I plan to graduate with an Associate degree as a Licensed Practical Nurse in May of 2000. After I graduate, I intend to work through the summer, and continue on next fall at Northland Community and Technical College in Thief River Falls, to pursue an Associate degree as a Registered Nurse. I have been working as a Nursing Assistant in long-term care for just over two and a half years, and I have become very comfortable working with the elderly. I have always been interested in the nursing field, but I was never sure exactly where I wanted to work after I was finished with school.

Being from a small town, there weren't very many options available in the field of nursing, other than a small nursing home and clinic. Since I had only experienced work in long-term care, I had always hoped that when I became a nurse, I could work elsewhere in a large hospital. I have always loved babies and little kids, so I thought that maybe I would enjoy working in either a family birthing center or in pediatrics. However, the further I advance in my classes, and the more clinical experiences I have, the more I see myself leaning back toward long-term care, the place I never thought I would want to be. By no means have I had negative clinical experiences working with small children. In fact, I would still like to work with them if given the opportunity some day. But there is something about working with the elderly that is so rewarding, and leaves you with such a feeling of satisfaction, knowing that you have made a difference. I never feel judged by them, and they have a way of making you feel so appreciated for the littlest things. I feel very comfortable with the routine of the nursing home, and I enjoy the relationships that one is able to build with each resident after working with them on a daily basis over time.

I come from a large family, being one of six children, and I feel that that has influenced my ability to communicate openly and to work well with others. I have lived in Warroad, a small rural town in northern Minnesota, for most of my life. All my grandparents live in Canada, so I rarely have the opportunity to see them. I know that if any of them became unable to care for themselves and had to resort to living in a nursing home, I would hope that the people caring for them would do all that they could to give them the best possible care. When I work with the elderly in the nursing home, I hope that I am able to give that care to someone else's parents or grandparents.

Nursing, to me, is one of the most important fields there is, in regards to service. I feel that it finds people who are the most desperate and at the most difficult point in their life, and is able to turn them around so they can continue on with their life. To be a part of that type of work makes me feel very proud, and I hope that I am able to contribute what I can to make that kind of difference.

Treasured Jewels

A year after Cathy's death, we received an envelope in the mail addressed to Cathy Watson. That, by itself, was enough to cause my heart to flutter, but this particular envelope was also addressed in Cathy's own handwriting. My emotions ran rampant, as I slit open the envelope and removed a single yellow piece of paper. As I unfolded it, I saw more of her handwriting and began to read the contents. I realized it was something she had written a year earlier while attending a seminar. It was a short memo entitled "Promises to Myself" and listed the five following things she was trying to incorporate into her life.

1. I will think of five things that I am thankful for every day

2. I will get to bed before midnight at least three nights a week

3. I will take twenty minutes a day to relax by myself

4. I will try to think of three nice things to say to someone every day

5. I will try not be such a perfectionist

Cathy Watson 10-28-1999

After Cathy's death, her personal belongings seemed almost sacred. I remember sorting through notebooks, textbooks, journals, diaries, backpacks, purses, anything that had belonged to her, with the hope that I might find something of value. It was not the things of monetary value that were of great worth, rather the little notes found stuffed between the pages of a book, the lists, the doodled pages in notebooks. Those bits and pieces gave a bird's eye view into her dreams and aspirations. They became the jewels— treasures, keepsakes, precious memories to hold on to.

Glimpses of What Cathy Meant to Her Sisters

Nine months after Cathy's death, Mark asked each of his daughters to write a few comments about what Cathy had meant to them. The following are a few excerpts;

"Those who truly knew and loved her may go on, but the mark Cathy left in our hearts will always be felt."

"There are some people who, when they die, the whole world seems depopulated. —Alphonse de Lamartine"

"With Cathy gone, things will never be quite the same. There's always that spark of energy missing, and her smile and that twinkle in her eyes just can't be matched. Sometimes I look at her pictures, and imagine she is right there in front of me. But I know that if she were there, I would be in tears from laughing too hard or learning one more way to touch people's lives."

"I look up to Cathy more than anyone else in the world. Anyone who knew her knows best that she had a heart of gold and that she would do anything to make someone else's life better."

"She was truly my role model. She was kind to the young, her peers, and the elderly. She treated everyone equally and brought joy to many peoples' hearts. She knew if something was wrong without ever asking."

A Tribute to Cathy by Her Dad

Cathy was a real prize and a real joy. She loved to make stupid, goofy faces just to make you laugh. She had a warm, accepting smile. She was a peacemaker. She had a passion for elderly people. She loved to dance. She had a servant's heart. The last couple of Bible studies Charity and Cathy had together were about the Good Samaritan, and her bookmark was in the last passage they were studying:

No one lights a lamp and puts it in a place where it will be hidden, or under a bowl. Instead he puts it on its stand, so that those who come in may see the light.(Luke 11:33 NIV).

We were first told that Catherine's name meant grace. Well, we've since found out it means purity. In our hearts, it will always mean grace. Her life on earth was grace personified. She graced us with her presence in a way that only Cathy could.

I look on Cath's earthly life with the fondness and pride of a father for a daughter who had made him proud. The memories I have of her bright and happy presence will be something I will treasure for the rest of my life here on earth.

Glimpses of Cathy through Jered's Eyes

The following is an excerpt from a college paper written by Jered in December 2000. It is included with Jered's permission.

What I learned most during my high school years was not taught in class. I learned how to love. I learned how to treat somebody for whom you really care. I learned about caring for someone so much you would do anything to make them happy and have them be the most important thing in my life. My girlfriend taught me how to take the good out of every situation rather than to be negative toward or criticize others for things they do. She taught me how not to be afraid to tell people how I really feel inside. She helped open my eyes to what is important in life. Even though I don't have her with me now, I will always have her with me in my heart. I didn't learn these things in school; I learned these things from my girlfriend. She taught me things far more important than I could learn in school.

Jered is a fine young man, who in spite of facing death at a vulnerable age, chose to move forward. He is now married to a beautiful, sensitive, young woman, and God has blessed them with two beautiful children. We are so proud of them, and they are a unique blessing in our lives. Joni, his wife, is the answer to our prayers, and their children, Connor and Cami, are precious reminders of God's faithfulness. I am confident that if Catherine can see down through the windows of heaven, she is sincerely happy for them.

What Remains

Many of us have heard great teaching, but most often, it doesn't remain with us. I believe what God does will remain! And what He doesn't do—won't! Rather obvious, but true![83]

Jesus says, "I am the true vine, and my Father is the gardener. Remain in me, and I will remain in you. No one can bear fruit by itself; it must remain in the vine. Neither can you bear fruit unless you remain in me. I am the vine; you are the branches. If a man remains in me and I in him, he will bear much fruit; apart from me you can do nothing." (John 15:1, 4-5 NIV).

"…And a little child will lead them."(Isaiah 11:6c NIV).

When our days are over, what will we leave behind? What things will remain? What will others remember most about our lives?

Cathy's life was short by our standards, yet in its brevity, she touched lives in ways that remain. My prayer is that these lasting things will draw others to a personal, living, vibrant relationship with Jesus Christ.

These following comments are from some of the cards and notes we received after the accident.

Carol (mother of Cath's best friend): *"I thank God for Cathy's life—it was so short and yet she made such an impact for good on everyone she was around."*

Susie (roommate during college): *"She brought sunshine to 406 Hamline. She was the most giving person I have ever known…"*

Friends from her hometown: *"May Cathy be remembered for her smile and unconditional love."*

John and Barb (parents of roommate): *"She was one of the most kind, generous and Spirit-filled people! Anyone who knew her was lucky that she touched their life."*

Shari (teacher and family friend): *"God used Cathy to reach a countless number of people with messages of hope and life. She is an awesome child of God…"*

Gwynn (Sunday school teacher): *"She was a lovely, kind, fun-loving addition always expressing sensitivity to those around her…"*

Judy (high school teacher):

"In my fourteen years of teaching, she was one of the brightest, creative, and most organized students I have ever had! Her compassion for people led her into nursing as a career. She was an exceptional young lady."

Melinda (director of nursing): *"Your daughter was an excellent nurse and person. She brought a positive cheerful attitude to the care center. She brought a special caring touch to both staff and residents. We are all better for having known and loved her."*

Linda (co-worker): *"There will be a void in the care center where only Cathy's enthusiasm would fill. It will be* a challenge to step up, take life a little less seriously, have a sense of humor, smile more, hug more, laugh more and love more. She taught us many things. But the greatest was to live as if tomorrow may never come."

Judy (co-worker): *"…what a true privilege to work with your daughter. … Her beautiful smile, kindness toward all residents and staff members and wonderful bubbly personality will be greatly missed."*

Delphine (resident): *"Your daughter was a very kind, gentle, person who took the time to be nice and talk to you."*

Mary (resident): *"Cathy was like a daughter to me, and I loved her."*

Lisa (director): *"Cathy was an exceptional employee and we all enjoyed working with her…"*

Gail (director of nursing) *"…when Catherine walked into a room the residents here lit up! What a wonderful presence she had. Please know she was highly respected."*

Jerry (professor): *"Catherine was a wonderful student and very deserving of the scholarship she received. Catherine's friendly smile and sincere love of everyone she met were a tribute to her family values and Christian life. Life is very fragile, and we must live each day showing our faith and love."*

Daphne (chair of the Dr. Sather Nursing Scholarship): *"We were so pleased to award her—commenting on how, today we seldom see such ideal candidates."*

Jennie (nursing instructor): *"She lived life to the fullest and filled everyone's life she touched. She was so humble. Her profound love for the elderly, her sincere attitude and her strong desire to do well were just a few of her many 'best nurse' qualities."*

Mary (nursing instructor): *"Her memory will continue to be a positive influence in all the lives she touched while here on earth."*

Barb (practical nursing director): *"Cathy's love will never be lost as she left so much of it with all who knew her."*

Duane (classmate): *"She was a positive caring person who taught me to live and capture every day."*

Christine (classmate): *"She was a brilliant woman. Her charm, attitude and smile would brighten a room just with her presence."*

Gone, But Not Forgotten

Cathy loved her nieces and coveted the occasions when she was able to spend quality one on one time with them. In the weeks before her death, Cathy had spent a lot of time with her niece, Ryan, who was then twenty-eight months old. Ryan loved to climb up on the piano bench beside her Auntie Cathy and wait for her to play her favorite songs. It was never too long before they were both singing and dancing around the living room like a couple of little kids.

Last year, when Ryan was nine years old, she had a question on a class assignment that asked who had inspired her most musically. She responded by saying, "my Auntie Cathy." What a treasure to know, that although Ryan was so young at the time of Cathy's death, she still has a distinct memory of her.

A Fiftieth Birthday Letter

For my fiftieth birthday, my husband and daughters planned a special party. As a gift, each one wrote me a letter thanking me for my role in their lives, and then together they wrote the following letter as though it were written by Cathy. I wept buckets of tears as I read it. It brought back many memories.

May 11, 2005

A letter to Mom from Cathy,

I would give anything to be with my family at your fiftieth birthday celebration and to throw my arms around you and say, "I love you, Mom. Happy fiftieth." I'm counting on Dad and my sisters to make my presence felt and to say for me some of the things I would say if I were there with you.

You are the reason behind the person I became. You possess the qualities that I admire and that I tried to develop in myself. You had a knack for knowing what to say and when not to say anything. You always made me feel special and gave me a sense of self-worth and self-confidence. You put us kids first. You listened, even when we said things you didn't really want to hear. You were my mom, but you were also like a best friend. You raised me to be able to stand on my own two feet and taught me the value of hard work. I feel blessed to have grown up in the family God gave me. My fondest memories are of times with family. I loved sharing my deepest thoughts and dreams with you. It meant so much to me when you came to Jered's cabin. I was so proud to give you homemade presents and to bake cookies for you and Dad and my sisters. You let me have friends over and always made them feel welcome, and you'd do special things like make caramel rolls or pancakes for us for breakfast. The reason I was able to care for the residents at the care center the way I did was because of what I learned from you and the things you did for others.

Remember when we didn't have much money and you'd make us clothes and bake crackers and bread and homemade soup and Cheez Whiz just to help us get by? Even when we didn't have much, I never felt gypped. You could make food taste so good even when you didn't have much to work with. We always knew there would be dinner on the table. I'm so grateful that I was raised in a Christian family. We saw God answering our prayers and providing for us, like the groceries that were left on the steps at Baylor and the money orders we'd get in the mail, braces on Laurie's teeth, and so many other ways.

Remember when you would hide Easter eggs around the house and you'd give us pails and we'd look all over the place trying to find them? You made home such a fun place to be.

Remember when we'd play hide and seek and end up scrunching in the kitchen cupboards and in all other kinds of crazy places in the house?

Remember when I stuck my pipe cleaner flower in the wall outlet to make my nicely cleaned up room look prettier and Christy was yelling, "Cathy's been elexacuted! Cathy's been elexacuted!" And you jumped over the baby gate to rescue me and ran cold water over the burns on my hands and cuddled me in your arms and comforted me. And I kept saying, "I'm not dead! I'm not dead!"

Remember when you'd make each of us our favorite kind of cake on our birthday? You always made birthdays so special. Even if we didn't have very much money, you would make our parties fun and give us the most meaningful gifts.

Remember when I was in Annie and you made me that pretty black velvet dress with the white frilly collar and red ribbon? And remember opening night was my birthday, and my name was on the Patch restaurant sign?

Remember when we talked about me breaking up with my boyfriend? What you don't know is that I talked with Keri and told her how easy it was to talk about "stuff like that" with you and that you were "cool about it."

Remember when you would come to football games, even though you had no idea what was happening on the field? You never missed one, you were always there cheering on the cheerleaders. You always made a point of coming to every special event I was involved in, whether it was for band, NHS, or cheerleading.

Remember when I had mono just before graduation? I was lying down in what is now Sarah's room, and you held a cool washcloth on my forehead and brought me chicken noodle soup. You would always take care of us when we were sick and do all those little things that showed how much you loved us. What you did for me made me want to be there for you and to tell you that if you ever got sick I would take care of you so you wouldn't have to go into a nursing home.

Remember when I graduated from high school, you put so much work into making my senior year fun for me? You put all of your creative juices into making my graduation party unique and special.

Remember when we'd go to Grand Beach and all the fun we'd have? Lying on the beach getting cooked like lobsters and goofing around on the floaties in the water; diving into the waves on those windy days; the games we played at night; the candy drawer; playing nickel bingo. You made it so much fun. Remember when Christy and I numbered all the different kinds of poop? Or when I was too scared to go outside so I just went to the bathroom in *a bucket in the kitchen? Do you remember me swimming with the buoy chasing me? Remember when we'd go to D.J.'s and you would give all of us money to play games and get a treat?*

Remember when you threw a surprise birthday party for me and no one came except Charity? You did all that work to make it nice for me and I know you were disappointed with my friends. But that didn't change what you did for me.

Remember when I babysat Savannah when she was a baby and she got a deep cut on her head? But you helped me take care of her and reassured me it wasn't my fault.

Remember when I would make brownies and they'd either get burnt or be raw in the middle? I'd always say, "Don't worry about the mess, Mom, I'll clean it up." But you usually ended up doing it. Sorry!

Remember when I'd tell stories from the care center? You were always eager to listen and laugh with me.

Remember the line dance I made up with Sarah for Homecoming and what a great job Sarah did in finishing it for me?

Remember when I would tell "would you rather" jokes? Or when I would do impersonations of Martha Mouse and Shaky Aggie? Or how about when I would joke about what I ate that day?

Remember when I was so anxious to come home from Grand Forks but somehow I took a wrong turn and ended up in Fargo? That was so annoying.

Remember when you would come to 406 Hamline and stay with me? I was always so proud to show you off to my friends so they'd know how lucky I was to have you as my mom. Thank you for all the special things you did for me and for helping me get through the tough times. You made them easier to bear.

Remember all the pictures you took of me for Frosty and Prom and Homecoming? Each event was so important to me and you made sure to make it special.

Remember when you and Dad came to Grand Forks for my Pinning Ceremony and you gave me those beautiful roses? I was so proud of what I had accomplished and that you were willing to be there to share it with me.

Remember I'd watch my favorite movies like Mystic Pizza, Clifford, Muriel's Wedding and Superstar and then act out the parts to make you laugh?

Remember when I'd dance around the living room with Ryan to "Lorie Line"?

Remember when we would talk wedding, marriage and babies? I would look so forward to weekends off and free days just to be with you and talk about stuff like that.

Remember when you got that letter in the mail after I died, that told about my goals? I had that all planned because I knew you'd need a little smile.

Remember when I would say "Duane the tub, I'm dwowning!"? Or when I wrote that paper on OCD and bulimia and the whole class thought it was the truth?

Remember when I would sit at the piano and play concerts while you were in the kitchen and Dad was in the garden? It meant so much to me that I could do something for you that you really liked.

That night before I passed away, you cooked me spaghetti with zucchini on it, but you were such a mother—sending me to my room to change out of my *good white nursing clothes. You were definitely born with the maternal instinct.*

You gave me life. You gave me love. You gave me the reason to be proud of being me because of all that you gave me from your heart. You took time for me during the day and tucked me in at night. I loved the made-up stories you'd tell me. You kissed my owies better. You always tried to be fair, and I respected your judgment on so many things. I wanted to be a mother just like you so that my children would have what I had. You are such a rock, Mom. Solid. Dependable. I always felt that my feet were on firm ground when I was around you. You were like my blankie that I pulled around as a baby that made me feel safe, protected, secure. The greatest treasure I have in heaven is the friendship we shared. You instilled in me the importance of honesty, like not cheating on my taxes, and integrity, to say and do the right thing, and to tell the truth, to be kind and not give up on anybody. The faith you demonstrated and the values you lived helped me to trust God and to make good decisions.

What you did for us defines the true meaning of love. People talk about love, but you showed by your actions what love is. It's giving without expecting anything in return. It's doing things for others even when you don't really want to or when they don't deserve it. It's going the extra mile to make things nice for someone.

Mom, it was the little things that you did that added up to the biggest thing you could do. I've never known a more caring, giving, and forgiving person in my life. You were willing to look past my faults and moodiness and sometimes even my rudeness and love me for me anyway.

Mom, you taught me so much about the blessing of sharing and giving and being kind and thoughtful even when deep down the feeling wasn't there. I am so thankful for my family. I so wish I could be there in person tonight.

God's greater purpose is what matters most, and that is for all of us to be thankful for each other and thoughtful of one another and willing to put the needs of others before our own. That's what family is all about—doing things for each other unselfishly and caringly because that's what makes for a strong family.

I love you, Mom.

Happy Birthday,
Cathy

Virtual Memorial's Website

Several months after Cathy's death, Keri set up a memorial on the Internet at www.virtualmemorials. com. This site became a place where family and friends could visit and post words of encouragement. To date the site has received over 27,000 hits.

The following two messages that were posted were particularly meaningful to us.

November 17, 2000

Cathy,

To a girl who had unlimited potential, a heart as big as the world, and a radiance that nobody else could quite embrace. Your sense of humor was incredible, and the talents you possessed were amazing, both musically and socially. God implanted in you so many beautiful things, all of which blossomed and came shining through your life. Your compassion was inescapable. I can't imagine Heaven compared to what it truly is. As the angels sing with you, and as you continue to experience the Eternal Life that is talked about but seldom realized as a reality, know the Love here you left behind is catchy in unspeakable volumes!

Love, A Classmate at WHS

February 12, 2002

I don't know where to start. A huge part of me misses Cathy. We weren't best friends and we didn't hang out a lot, but we did get the best of that little bit o' life from each other. We shared inside jokes and laughed together. I always looked at her as you would look at "the person who has everything." Though it wasn't the material things you would associate first with that phrase, it was the greatest things in life. A super nice family, a great smile with the ability to make anyone happy, talent, talent, talent, niceness, bravery, intelligence, and undying faith, everything I would want from life. To say that she was a role model for the people around her is an understatement.

I think what happened to Cathy is such a rare accident, that it's only fitting. Cathy is a rare person. The tragedy wouldn't sound right if she had died from old age or poison or even in the WTC attacks. God knows that in those short nineteen years, Cathy did more for community, world, and life in general than she needed to, than most people will ever accomplish. I do not write what I think I have to, I write what is true and how I feel. Cathy was a blessing to the world. That is all anyone needs to know. Everyone who has ever met her knows exactly what I am saying. I truly believe she was too good for this place anyway. She was an angel in the flesh, I wish the rest of the world could have seen it for themselves. So to Cathy's family, I believe God picked you because He knew you could handle it. I am sorry for your loss. And though I may not know to what depths your pain and grief goes, I have some of my own. And more importantly, like you I have lot of great memories.

Leah

Contact Information

Deb Watson

PO Box 45

Warroad, MN 56763-0045

218-386-3228

www.debwatson-kissgoodbye.com

markwat@mncable.net

End Notes

[1] 2Ti 1:12 NIV

[2] William Barry, *God's Passionate Desire and Our Response,* (Notre Dame, IN: Ave Maria Press, 1993), 87.

[3] Brennan Manning, *The Rabbi's Heartbeat,* (Colorado Springs, CO: NavPress, 2003), 79.

[4] Jn 3:29a NIV

[5] Mt 10:19b-20 NIV

[6] Ac 4:29b NIV

[7] Merton P. Strommen and A. Irene Strommen, *Five Cries of Grief,* (Minneapolis, MN: Augsburg Fortress Publishers, 1996), 33.

[8] Nicholas Wolterstorff, *Lament for a Son,* (Grand Rapids, MI: Wm B Eerdmans Publishing Co., 1987), 14–15.

[9] *Encarta Dictionary: English (North America) Microsoft Office Word*

[10] 2Co 12:9 NIV

[11] Manning, *The Rabbi's Heartbeat,* 117.

[12] Mt 21:22 NIV

[13] Jn 14:27 NIV

[14] Isa 40:31 NIV

[15] Ro 5:3–4 NIV

[16] Gerald Sittser, *A Grace Disguised,* (Grand Rapids, MI: Zondervan Publishing House, 1995), 86.

[17] Ps 56:8 NASV

[18] Rev 21:4 NIV

[19] Larry Crabb, *Shattered Dreams,* (Colorado Springs, CO: Waterbrook Press, 2001), 122.

[20] Ps 25:4 NIV

[21] Ro 12:2 NIV

[22] Ro 12:2 NIV

[23] Larry Crabb, *Finding God,* (Grand Rapids, MI: Zondervan Publishing House, 1993), 29.

[24] A. W. Tozer, *"The Pursuit of God,"* Chapter 5 http://www3.calvarychapel.com/library/Tozer-AW/PursuitOfGod/05.htm (accessed February 9, 2009).

[25] Jer 29:13 NIV

[26] 1Co 3:11 NIV

[27] Norman L. Geisler, *Systematic Theology*, (Grand Rapids, MI: Bethany Book House Publishing, 2003), 2:536.

[28] Sittser, *A Grace Disguised*, 179.

[29] Mt 28:18 NIV

[30] Jn 8:32 NIV

[31] Lk 22:45 NIV

[32] Ac 8:2 NIV

[33] Lk 23:43 NIV

[34] ICo 2:9b NIV

[35] Jn 14:2 NIV

[36] 1Th 4:13–18 NIV

[37] Rev 22 NIV

[38] Manning, *The Rabbi's Heartbeat*, 55.

[39] Billy Graham, *Angel: God's Secret Agents*, (Markham, ON: Pocket Books, a division of Simon & Schuster, Inc., 1977), 49.

[40] Dr. David Jeremiah, *What the Bible Says about Angels*, (Sisters, OR: Multnomah Publishers, Inc., 1996), 22.

[41] Ibid., 24.

[42] Ibid., 22.

[43] C. Fred Dickason, *Angels, Elect and Evil*, (Chicago, IL: Moody Press, 1975), 97–101.

[44] Jas 4:2b–3 NIV

[45] Mt 25:21 NIV

[46] Jn 7:38 NIV

[47] Mt 22:37 NIV

[48] Mk 12:33 NIV

[49] Brennan Manning, *The Wisdom of Tenderness*, (New York, NY: Harper Collins Publisher, 2002), 48.

[50] Jehu Burton, *Trusting through Tears*, (Grand Rapids, MI: Baker Book House, 2000), 145.

[51] Source unknown

[52] Larry Crabb, *The Safest Place on Earth*, (Nashville, TN: Word Publishing, 1999), 5.

[53] Jn 15:11 NIV

[54] Ro 12:12 NIV

[55] Crabb, *The Safest Place on Earth*, 39.

[56] Ps 33:8 NIV

[57] Ps 119:49–50 NIV

58 Job 30:27 NIV

59 Ro 9:2 NIV

60 1Pe 4:12 NIV

61 Jn 9:3 NIV

62 Jas 1:2–4 NIV

63 Sittser, *A Grace Disguised,* 154.

64 Bob Stacey, *A Father's Tears*, (Joplin, MO: College Press Publishing Co., 1998), 32.

65 Ibid., 93.

66 Joseph Bayly, *The Last Thing We Talk About,* (Elgin, IL: David C. Cook Publishing, 1973), 105.

67 H. Norman Wright, *Experiencing Grief,* (Nashville, TN: Broadman & Holman Publishers, 2004), 83.

68 Ps 23 NIV

69 Lyrics from "I Believe in a Hill Called Mount Calvary," William J Gaither, Gloria Gaither and Dale Oldham

70 Brent Curtis and John Eldredge, *The Sacred Romance, Drawing Closer to the Heart of God,* (Nashville, TN: Thomas Nelson, 1997), 137.

71 Crabb, Larry, *Shattered Dreams,* 87.

72 Mt 16:26a NIV

73 Brennan, *The Rabbi's Heartbeat*, 85.

74 Mk 6:31–32 NIV

75 Mt 11:28–30 NIV

76 Zep 3:17 NIV

77 Ro 2:11 NIV

78 2Pe 3:9 NIV

79 Randy Alcorn, *Safely Home,* (Carol Stream, IL Tyndale House Publishers, Inc., 2001), 1.

80 *Threads of Love*, Lori Line, "Lori Line Live," Time Line Productions, Inc., 1996, compact disc. is a piano piece composed by Lorie Line and introduced to us by Cathy.

81 Alcorn, *Safely Home,* 201.

82 Lk 12:34 NIV

83 Email from Cara Morrison 5/22/07

CPSIA information can be obtained
at www.ICGtesting.com
Printed in the USA
LVOW05s1444080817

544250LV00005B/657/P